TRANSFORMING GRACE

By Anne, a lay apostle

TRANSFORMING GRACE

By Anne, a lay apostle

ISBN: 978-1-940737-22-5

Library of Congress Number: applied for

Publisher: Direction for Our Times

In Ireland:
Direction for Our Times
The Hague Building
Cullies
Cavan
Co. Cavan
Ireland

In the USA:
Direction for Our Times
9000 West 81st Street
Justice, IL 60458
USA

www.directionforourtimes.org

Direction for Our Times is a 501(c)(3) tax-exempt organization.

Manufactured in the United States of America.

How to Pray the Rosary information is used with permission. Copyright © Congregation of Marians of the Immaculate Conception, Stockbridge, MA 01263. www.marian.org.

Paintings of *Jesus Christ the Returning King* and *Our Lady Queen of the Church* by Janusz Antosz

V11.14

Nihil Obstat: Very Rev. John Canon Murphy, PP, VF

Imprimatur: ✠ Most Rev. Leo O'Reilly,
　　　　　　　　Bishop of Kilmore, Ireland

I dedicate this book to my husband,
James Joseph Clarke, with gratitude.

Table of Contents

Introduction

In the context of contemporary culture, it must be accepted that most of us are living with something we can call 'silence poverty'. Because of this, our thinking can be unruly. In order to become thoughtful men and women of God, we will have to find silence, begin to ponder and next make decisions about what goes into our minds. Then we must be disciplined about those decisions. We must not think for a moment that our actions and interactions are unaffected by our thoughts. We know the opposite is true. Therefore, all must be invited to greater discipline of thought.

If we need extreme graces to change negative and unholy patterns of thought, God will help us. Often the smallest action of the day is the most heroic and contemporary apostles who reclaim and then hold their minds for God's wishes will became saints as we are all meant to be saints.

As a reflection, we ask ourselves the following question. Am I actively practicing the application of holiness concepts each day? When do I contemplate which concepts I find challenging of late? My friends, if we are not practicing the application of holiness concepts each day, we risk reaching our full potential as apostles.

Currently, in terms of holiness, the primary battle ground must be the mind.

Yes, most of us suffer from some level of mind pollution, meaning, undisciplined and impulsive thoughts and thinking patterns and that is why we must make a decision and commit to becoming thoughtful. We are going to have to work hard to become thoughtful men and women of God. And then we will have to use discipline to remain thoughtful men and women of God. And at the beginning of this process, we may have to accept that some of the things we are using to entertain ourselves are inconsistent with holiness and may be creating patterns of thought that are inconsistent with Christ.

Are we humble and forgiving? Or do we hold grudges? Are we doing an inventory of our thoughts each day? Asking ourselves the hard questions?

Perhaps one hundred years ago this state of thoughtfulness occurred naturally, in a time before relentless noise. But contemporary man is addicted to noise and our listening sense is overused to the degree that when we should be listening attentively, for example listening to people, we cannot, will not or do not. We may categorize the words and communications from others, including our loved ones, in the same way we categorize the constant backtrack playing everywhere of words and music. We may have adapted to constant noise by listening only casually, as in, 'Are these words and music entertaining to me? Stimulating? Exciting to me? If not, I will tune them out, even as I pretend to listen.' We may have lost the ability to be selective in what we are attentive to and we may have lost the ability to use our listening sense for learning how to grow in holiness and learning how to love God's children around us.

It is no surprise that Jesus instructed this apostolate to promote compassionate listening as our third charism.

Silence poverty, or, constant noise, presents a truly special challenge for faithful people in this time. And along with the listening sense, we must also consider the sense of sight. Because, my friends, God's little children are watching images of God's little children being assaulted, humiliated and degraded and most would comment after viewing violence or disordered actions, 'It does not bother me.' But it does bother us. It has to. Because images of violence are more consistent with behaviors from hell than behaviors from heaven. And I believe that has an impact on the well-being of the mind, and, as a follow on, the well-being of the body and also society.

Thoughtful men and women of God must begin to distinguish the difference between our current culture and the way God wants us to live. And then we must strive to help our culture to look more like the culture of heaven. We are here on earth to learn about love and to help bring about God's Kingdom. We are here on earth to create conditions of peace and harmony around us. Imperfectly, yes it is true, but we, apostles, should be developing positively in the world, not receding into degeneration. And while we may excuse ourselves by saying, 'I cannot do anything about war or poverty in a third world country,' it must be stated that one thoughtful man or woman of God who contemplates God's will can avert war and can prompt or participate in a campaign to feed large numbers of people. And, at the very least, one thoughtful man or woman of God can stake out a safe pasture for Jesus in his or her mind where there is order, purity and kindness.

Because, if we are amongst those who have normalized the participation in pornography or graphic violence, (watching is participating), then we will miss our cues for God in the world. And through these past-times we are saying more about our wounds and pain than we are saying about anything else. If we are addicted to something we must contemplate ourselves honestly. Ask why. Why am I doing this when I know it is bad for me and that it hurts others?

What we do is important. Each one of us is important. Listen carefully to the truth. God is counting on us. We must pray contemplatively each day. What do we miss, my friends, about ourselves and others because we are rushing through life?

It is worth wondering.

Now, how does this unruliness of mind affect our representation of the Gospel message? Possibly, we get stuck on the letter of the law as the Pharisees did. Possibly, we project our own limited thinking onto the Gospel Message because of a dearth of true holy contemplation. This could cause us to view people dualistically, as either all bad or all good when we know that in truth people are generally good and they also make mistakes, sometimes big mistakes over long periods of time.

We look to St. Paul for guidance as to how we should present the Gospel message.

"Do not forget that you had no Christ and were excluded from membership of Israel, aliens with no part in the covenants with their Promise; you were immersed in this world, without hope and without God. But now, in Christ Jesus, you that used to be so far apart from us have been brought very close, by the blood of Christ. For he is the peace between us, and has made the two into one and broken down the barrier which used to keep them apart, actually destroying in his own person the hostility caused by the rules and decrees of the Law. This was to create one single New Man in himself out of the two of them and by restoring peace through the cross, to unite them both in a single Body and reconcile them with God. In his own person he killed the hostility. Later he came to bring the good news of peace, peace to you who were far away and peace to those who were near at hand. Through him, both of us have in the one Spirit our way to come to the Father. So you are no longer aliens or foreign visitors: you are citizens like all the saints, and part of God's household" (Ephesians 2:12 22).

Saint Paul references hostility caused by the rules and decrees in the time of our Lord. Where is that happening today? We, if we are preaching the legitimate Gospel message, will be treating people as potential citizens of heaven, brothers and sisters on a journey. If we focus on love, we will usually provoke less hostility in those struggling with the 'rules and decrees' because when we speak with compassion for the circumstances of another, God usually, eventually, wins the campaign.

Perhaps it is only Our Lady, as Queen of the Church, who can help us to both order our minds to heaven and also strike the right note in offering God's love to others.

Prayer to Our Lady Queen of the Church

Oh Mary, mother of Jesus and Queen of the Church, I ask you to bless me with fidelity to my vocation. Assist me in seeing that my service, however humble and hidden, is important to the universal Church. Strengthen me in times of trial and watch over my family and loved ones. Help me, beloved mother, to remain faithful to Jesus Christ, your son, the Returning King. Amen.

Locutions from
St. Francis of Assisi

April 2, 2011
St. Francis

Dearest Anne, thank you for your attention. Distractions are manifold in the spiritual life, particularly when God has a project that is important to Him. Anne, this project is important to God and I am your helper. In my time, my instruction was clear. God asked me to rebuild His Church and in my human and limited thinking, I began at once, not knowing or understanding the scope of the instruction or how I would suffer for its fulfillment. Holiness is what is needed in the Church, true holiness that has, as its foundation, advancement in virtue. You must be very humble and small and speak very volubly about this fact. Why does the Church suffer? Because she lacks holiness. If the Church was as holy as she needed to be, she would not feel the persecutions. Because the Church became lukewarm in many areas, those who were destructive proceeded more or less unchecked as they sowed seeds into the foundation of the Church which weakened her. Do I blame any one man? No. I do not. And God will not, even while He will hold each man accountable for the damage done through his iniquities. Anne, do I speak with a harsh Spirit? No. I do not. I speak with Truth and that means in union with God's Holy Spirit. Anne, you must urge the people to advance into virtue. You must urge the Church to become holier. Less business, more prayer, Anne. That is what will happen anyway so best the Church be prepared by divesting herself of her worldliness and robing herself again in her heavenly garb, that is, prayer. Apostles must be informed that this is their instruction from God. We will reclaim the Church for God through holiness in the Church and that call must go out to every single follower of Jesus Christ.

3

Sunday April 3, 2011
St. Francis

Anne, you are being distracted. When you are ill, you must redouble your efforts to remain detached from distraction. Focus on your duty, as much as you are able to perform it, and focus on the things you know Jesus wills for you, for example, recording for me. That was the right decision and an example of rejecting the alternative, which would be to allow the distraction to draw you into upset. That is just a friendly word from the brother who loves you and sees your distress. Distractions suck joy from a day like liquid through a straw. I became very adept at identifying them and I will pray for that for you, too.

Back to the Church and the need to reclaim it. You must see, Anne, that there is very little discussion of holiness concepts. You must see how those who have been called to draw the Church along are treated. While this resistance has always been present, this time presents an additional obstacle. That obstacle is moral lassitude. "Yes, they're attacking us but if we defend the truth we will be hacked to pieces." Anne, dearest, let me say that we must be willing to be hacked to pieces, literally or figuratively, in the name of the Gospel. The message is always gentle but always true and always complete. I speak not to put arrows in the quivers of those who shoot at trembling sinners. I speak to put arrows in the quivers of those who target distortion. I speak to put arrows in the quivers of those who target inconsistencies in obedience. 'I am obedient and yet I work actively against the Church?' There is no love in this, no commitment to truth. There is no desire for advancement according to the Spirit. The Spirit is denounced in many, or distorted to the degree that it is weak and bound. When this happens, when the Spirit is not welcomed in its fullness of power, the Spirit bursts forth through another receptacle.

April 5, 2011
St. Francis

It is good that you urge the people to holiness. Tell them that if they truly amend their lives and become holy, others will follow their example and the Renewal can begin coming through them in ways they could not have imagined. While this is occurring, there are others around the world doing the same thing. The prayer groups are providing pockets of commitment to holiness. Little groups of followers, scattered here and there, have great power. Our Church has always been renewed this way, over the years, and our Church began this way. Do not underestimate what you are about. When someone comes into service, thank God. When someone leaves service, thank God. That was my approach and it helped me to retain equilibrium through every experience. All is joy when you work for Jesus. God's creation gives joy. People are carrying burdens, and they need love. God's creation caresses our spirits. If you want to know a secret, I will tell you. When I could not be away on my own, I closed my eyes and allowed God to caress my spirit in the same way. I would recall other moments in time from heaven. This will help you. All love surrounds you and flows through you to others. I will be with you today.

Sunday April 10, 2011
St. Francis

Ah, the painful process of observing where the Church needs healing...this is what apostles are experiencing. God often shows people where the need is in the Church by allowing people to experience it. This is what happened with me. Perhaps one suffers from the weakness of a person in the Church. After dealing with one's wound, one should move to illuminate and remedy the weakness. We should not run from weaknesses in the Church. That would be a childish and limited response. We must not walk away from our obligations or run from adversity. We, apostles, are amongst those who benefit from adversity by allowing it to teach us. We lead with calm confidence in Christ. Point out God's creation everywhere. Rejoice that heaven has favored you, even though it is costing you. Do not allow adversity to drag you around. Submit completely to God. I will help.

April 11, 2011
St. Francis

We are moving into another time. Why are you so concerned about the virtues, Anne? I want you to think hard. God is looking for a renewal in the Church. People hear you speak about renewal and they think, "Yes, all of those people should come back and behave properly, like us." They do not think, "God's Spirit wants to renew the face of the earth beginning with me." Do you see?

One holy person who moves toward Christ with seriousness, despite his age or vocation, can bring many along with him. But there is complacency, meaning, to be clear, "I am working for Christ for some time and I am quite busy doing holy work therefore I have no need for serious self-examination and change." Anne, this attitude is pervasive in the Church on earth right now. You must urge each soul to go down deeply into his own self, into his sinfulness and that which is problematic in his soul. This humanity you point to, quite rightly, is messy, it is true, but it is up to the man to put order on it, through his cooperation with Christ. I never ceased striving for greater holiness. This is how you must urge the Church to greater holiness. If there is to be Renewal, it is going to have to begin with the people who are safely in the Church and be combined with those outside of the Church who are experiencing an aching need for God. The combination will provide favorable conditions for success.

So, I have given you a writing instruction for the day. You cannot abandon the Church because it needs to be reclaimed, Anne. That would be like me never picking up the first stone when the Church needed to be rebuilt. Sometimes, it is true, you can be overwhelmed by the scope of the need but if you do a little, God can do a lot.

Your humanity is the vehicle of the water. You are a fountain. What if a fountain picked itself up and walked away from the source of the water. It would cease to be a fountain. Its function would be defunct.

April 13, 2011
St. Francis

The groaning of the Church as she pushes herself out of one period and into another can be heard through all of heaven. In the lives of the saints, we see suffering of every sort. The saints will always have much to bear because through their willingness God sends graces for the times. When God is allowed to have His way with one of His created ones, He uses the opportunity for the good of humanity. Anne, we must develop more fountains in the Church. There must be many more who understand what it is to be a fountain of grace for others. Teaching, Anne, teaching is what will accomplish this for the Church. Do people need idle conversations about the Church and her leaders? No. People need pure teaching that will direct them to the heart of Christ and what is to be found there. And then they need firm parameters within which to evaluate their behaviors. Where will these parameters be found? In the Catechism. Anne, the Catechism is a catchment of truth. Use it for the apostolate. Pour it out over the apostles so that they are drenched in it. You will see. Your efforts will take off because God Himself directs your course. I am pleased with you and I will see that you have all of the help you need during this period of suffering.

May 3, 2011
St. Francis

Anne, do not be distracted, either by what others think of you or by your doubts about your holiness. God Himself will see to your soul. Do you believe me? Or do you doubt me? I am telling you the truth, Anne, and you must believe that God, in His love and mercy, will care for you tenderly.

About the Church, we should be about His business. The Catechism is gaining your attention because I am relentlessly putting it in front of you. I am confirming it for you again and again. Begin an initiative in teaching it and we will ignite it with heaven's fire. Heaven's fire is the fire of spread, Anne, and you watch as your apostolate, fueled by the fire of heaven, spreads across the world. All you have to do to reclaim the Church is serve. If you serve each day, the Church will begin to resemble itself again. The Church is pure. The Church is dynamic. The Church is always offering a response to the world, a response which redirects attention to God and His desires for His children. If, today, you feel discouraged, allow me to direct you back into simplicity. Anne, dearest, if you did not have enemies people would wonder how you escaped opposition. Opposition is not bad for you. It can be a barrier which propels you back into the center stream of the Church. Go right down the middle, Anne. Use the writings God has sent through you to comfort people and use the Catechism to teach people. Trust Me. I will steer you if you let me.

Visions of the Church

Today the Lord drew me into an experience that He wanted me to record. I became aware, gradually, of a space where children played. The sounds and general atmosphere were consistent with a pre-school or summer camp. I saw an area and realized it was outside. I saw grass and understood that the grass indicated a boundary and that these interactions were confined to this area. I was being allowed to observe what was taking place. I understood that this was a place of previous visions, that is, the area outside of the humble building that is the Church.

The Lord urged me to open my eyes fully and I understood that the people were not children, although there were several groups that included teenagers and even younger people. All were fully engaged in the work of their group and while they were aware of others, they interacted specifically with those assembled to work on whatever project belonged to them. To be clear, all were fully engaged with their own work but aware that they were working in a space which included others working on different projects.

Jesus made me aware of the lightness in the Spirit between them. These people were able to use their unique talents and gifts on the projects assigned to them by heaven and they contributed to their projects according to their strengths. This was significant because part of the reason the people were happy was because they were working to their strengths as opposed to being compelled to serve in ways that did not use their unique gifts. This is not a right, as I saw it, but a good way of proceeding in the space of creativity that is the Church.

I see this, the space that is the Church, as a mystical area which is meant to be safe for us. The projects I saw people working on seemed to include their service to the Church. The groups of people assembled to work together on particular projects possessed a marked freedom of interaction. The freedom was available because these individuals allowed each other to live Undefended Lives. There was no evidence of anyone pouncing on the flaws of those around them. They reminded me of children because of the openness and acceptance they had for each other.

At one group, a member began to sneeze. All waited patiently while the person gathered himself together after the fit of sneezing. There was no irritation, no surprise that the person would begin to sneeze, just patient acceptance and respect that while this person stopped the group quite often with his sneezing, he offered important contributions and the sneezing was not his fault but a part of the humanity that had been allowed for him by the Creator, his handicap, as it were.

The sneezing represents our humanity and the acceptance of the group indicated our acceptance of each other, with both our flaws and our genius. Everybody counts in this space and I saw that everyone's contribution should be reverenced.

There were spontaneous eruptions of laughter in some groups and as I saw that this was how it was supposed to be in the Church, I could not help but compare it to what is, at times, the reality. When I wondered what to do about this, it occurred to me that I could help to establish this type of atmosphere in our Apostolate as a service to heaven and a way of modeling for others. This does not feel burdensome because of the team assembled by God who desires this same experience of light-hearted service.

November 14, 2011

I was brought down into the Church yard again and I could hear the sound of happy voices. The Lord took me to a group working near the front yard of the Church, the furthest outer area. There a group worked, concentrating together on creating things intended to be floated over the line where our Church leaves off and other Christian faith communities begin. I watched this group for a while and could see that the Lord is very serious about this work. He wants this work done and He is prepared to send many inspirations.

My mystical friend showed me something very important. I saw that this group worked right on this side of the line. I saw the white line as the boundary, like the line on a tennis court. The significant part of this was that when my eyes were drawn down close to the group, I saw that there was the slightest space separating the work of this group from the boundary of the Church. They are not on the line. They are firmly on this side of the line with room to spare, meaning, no compromise with truth, I would think.

I saw the imprint of another group, one I suspect went before this group who were charged with working on the same project. They went over the white line and they then became ineffective. They did not accept that they were ineffective, rather, they aggressively insisted on their position of being over the line as righteous.

At any rate, this type of attitude from those in the Church is discordant for the ones remaining firmly fixed in the Church yard but eventually they die out, much like the ones who set up camps on the side of the living stream of grace flowing through the Church. They do not stand the test of time or leave imprints which will remain. I saw the imprint of those who had gone before them, who had crossed the line, gradually fading, not to be reclaimed. This is in contrast to the imprint of those who remain faithfully within the Church yard. Any imprint we leave can be quickly reclaimed by those who come after, even if it is taken by a storm of attack.

Jesus asked me to study these men and I did. I could see that they were holy. He told me that he would prefer that only men who had the ability to self-examine be put to work on this project.

I am understanding this project as ecumenism. But those who do not self-examine are terribly vulnerable to being drawn off target through a desire to see their work bear visible and immediate fruit. This flawed desire is stronger than their desire to allow God to earn the trust of the ones on the other side. He earns trust by providing them with good example. Good example is provided only through those who both have the teaching and the *theory* of the teaching absorbed into their souls. God said directly that He preferred less learning to holiness in this regard and that the people chosen to serve in this way should be only those who were abandoned to Him personally.

I saw what they were fashioning. My goodness. These light-filled ornaments were like balloons or beautiful Chinese lanterns in that they floated out of their hands, over the line and into the other faith communities. They were delicately fashioned with extreme care and love. They possessed, as their essence, the Christian truths that we, as Catholics, have in common with other Christian denominations. They were collected and welded together with the most current Church teachings. What comes to mind are Vatican II documents on the laity as well as the Papal encyclicals that incorporate teachings on love and sexuality. With these 'new' teachings we will be able to show the proper Christian response to the times. These teachings reflect the Spirit God is sending now and it is this teaching which will unite us to the other Christian denominations. The word current is very important here. Current in the Church can mean anything I suppose but I would think of it as 'untaught' or not adequately celebrated yet.

To summarize, ecumenism is very important to Christ. The people chosen to work on this should be more in possession of holiness than intellectual ability and they have to stay on this side of the Church line to be effective. Jesus showed me that when they crossed the line they instantly lose all effectiveness for His purposes. I want to clarify that being intellectual is not a handicap but sometimes, the most intellectual is not the person for a job of sensitivity because an intellectual, by the very nature of the well-developed side of the brain, might be less adept at sensitivity. I am not trying to insult anyone but I cannot let this drop as it was important and will be perhaps important to someone, someday.

November 15, 2011

Today I was drawn down into the yard and became gradually aware of the work and sound of the activities in the Church. Suddenly I heard a shout go up from a group and I looked over. They were so happy. Their work had experienced a triumph and they were joyful and triumphant. This was good and God was happy with them.

Then I felt my eyes drawn back to the group of religious sisters who offered their daily works each day in unison. They, too, experienced celebrations and joys but they saw each day as equally beneficial to God. This is a concept with which I want to deal gently because, Lord have mercy, nobody should try to take away our triumphs in the Church, given that service is often so painful. But we must view each day as a triumph.

God would like that group to see that they are successful on the days when their work appears to be going well and on the days when their work appears to be failing and at risk. God does not care. It is His affair. What Jesus liked about the people celebrating was their individual perseverance together on the task and their commitment to loving each other and working in union. This is a very different vision than we each have, it must be stated. We definitely can view success/failure differently than Jesus views it in terms of our service in the Church.

I asked Jesus to tell me what these triumphant ones were working on and He said they were working on service to a group of God's children who were literally starving to death in great numbers. This bodily hunger issue is very important to God. He does not like to see people dying of starvation and I know that conditions sometimes result in this and there is nothing anyone can do about it but I also see Jesus looking at large groups starving and His eyes are not on them but on those of us not suffering physical hunger. In other words, I see Jesus looking at people with food and in His eyes I see the people who have no food. He is willing us to help and to continue helping. He would say, ***"Perhaps you cannot solve the whole problem, but perhaps you can contribute to the cause in the smallest way. Do something and you will have***

honored My pain at seeing the Father's children suffer from hunger."

At any rate, He is immensely grateful to this group who actively love God's children suffering from hunger. He is also, today, using them as an example of rejoicing when work is objectively successful in a way which can be humanly measured. He would say to us, though, that He was as pleased with them when their work appeared to be failing as He is today when their work is clearly coming to a sublimely graceful outcome consistent with the beatitudes. This group has fed the hungry, may God bless them forever.

Back to the religious sisters in community, how consoling they are to view in this vision. We should take their example and move it into married life and the diocesan priesthood. They are all about rhythmic steady service and this keeps them peaceful. I can see Jesus looking at them and His eyes are filled with tenderness. Their hands are busy about work all day (work meaning whatever this order is called to by their God-given charisms) and at the end of the day they offer it to the Father through Jesus and He is glorified and the Father is accepting graciously of that which gives Him mercy for others.

I want to say the Father is calmed but that implies that He is not calm which is untrue. I want to say mollified but He is not like a petulant child. Perhaps the Father, when He receives the fidelity and constancy of these sisters, is moved to accept their offering and then return it to humanity as the purest grace, grace which consoles people despite God being rejected by them.

The key to this vision is dependability. These religious sisters are dependable. Their work is constant. Their love is raised to heaven at the end of each day as an offering of unity. The sisters themselves would not completely see their dignity or beauty. I think the sisters would independently feel they are unworthy or unable of this type of offering. That would be because they are consumed at times with their human frailties and temptations. Who is not? But they are part of something bigger and the truth that they remain in place as part of this camp of beautiful offering means that the enterprise keeps working, like a well bringing up water day after day. The fact that those drawing it up may feel tired, cantankerous, afraid, sad about their condition, etc. has no affect whatsoever on the truth that the water is being drawn up each day. They are part of something enormous and they should have courage!

They would have courage if they saw their offering as I see it today.

Back to the ecumenical team, I see them creating the most beautiful ornaments. I see these efforts as large light-filled lanterns, intricately decorated and shaped. Really…these are works of art. These constructions are then floated over the boundary to the other Christian denominations whose eyes are drawn upwards. There is a lot of silence necessary. More examples and less dialogue are needed, it seems to me.

The ones designing and launching these works are so humble and hopeful. God will honor their hope and they should be full of hope. I see them standing in the Church yard, on this side of the line, watching as the others watch the lanterns floating by. As they study the reaction, they are inspired to create another one, with a subtle difference, perhaps, a small additional swirl or a dainty adjustment. They are truly both studiers and artisans of the Catholic tradition.

A great painter does not create a bowl of fruit, but he studies the bowl of fruit in order to do justice to the integrity of the essence of the fruit he paints. He studies, contemplates and only then paints. This is why the Lord is saying that he prefers a holy man to a learned man on this topic because one who is a scholar but who has not contemplated the truths of our faith interiorly, evidencing application of these truths in his life, will not be able to give an accurate depiction of the truths to others. The master artist studies the fruit in all different lights and then decides how to actually illustrate the beauty of the fruit for others. The artist has tasted the fruit and loved it and that is why he is painting it at all. If he hated avocados and they filled him with revulsion, he would choose a different subject.

So, too, the man who is cynical about the Church must be the worst person in it to work on ecumenical matters.

I have seen both representations. Imagine the cynical one like an artist who is called to paint fruit. He paints a rotten apple, smashed against the ground in harsh light with ants crawling on it. Is this honoring the beauty of the apple? And yet, he paints on. Better he understand that this image does not accurately represent the dignity of the fruit God created for His children. Now, it is true that possibly he was given an apple like this once and possibly his pain must be honored in order for him to recover, however, he is the not the best one to teach others about the purpose and beauty of fruit, particularly apples.

Be alert if you are called to make decisions about the men and women serving in ecumenical matters. Choose wisely the people chosen to build bridges and be certain they possess fidelity to and understanding of Church teachings.

About bridges, I could see clearly that the bridge, where it is constructed, should draw people from outside of the line over into the Church yard. People in the Church yard are not intended to cross over and remain out. It is enough that they understand the flora and fauna on the other side. It is enough that they welcome those from the other side into the Church yard.

Of course we learn so much from people in other Christian denominations and indeed in other faiths entirely. Which Catholic has not witnessed the joyful praise and worship of other Christian denominations and found himself inspired and lifted up? Which Catholic has not admired the grasp of Scripture evidenced in other faiths? Which Catholic has not been impressed with the courage and stamina of our brothers and sisters working in mission fields filled with hostile elements?

There is no real conflict between us and we must learn all that we can from other Christians, but we draw it into our tradition and fashion it accordingly. God wants us to retain our identity and teach it. He does not need us to abandon our identity. It is a beautiful identity, filled with hope for God's children on earth.

November 16, 2011

Today I was drawn into the Church yard and I rested in the industrious sound of people working. From where I sat, I expected to see the humble, small but beautiful Church in front of me and yes, it was there, but it was oh so far away. I looked to my left and right and saw that a vast area stretched between the boundaries meaning that the Church's area of influence was very large indeed. Additionally, as I began to study groups of people, I saw, for example, a group of Dominican sisters in one area, then I looked at a different place and saw another group. They were identifiable to me because of their habits and their rhythmic way of serving God, which Jesus loved. But I saw that these were of different nationalities and Jesus said, "Use the words international representation."

I saw that there is international representation in the Church which means that while various countries may appear a bit different as they inculcate the teachings of the Church and combine these teachings with their culture and cultural beliefs, the same movement, meaning 'way of serving' is true throughout. I understood that for it to be the way Jesus desires, we must absorb Church teaching and adapt it to our culture carefully.

Leaders of international movements must be certain that each country's individual leadership has correctly absorbed the spirituality. Perhaps I should say, has had the *opportunity* to correctly absorb the spirituality because, while we cannot insure that anyone serve according to the Holy Spirit, there should be ongoing evaluation to ascertain that membership is accurately reflecting the founder's intent. This oversight is crucial to the Lord and I believe He wants this subject examined. This would probably be important for renewal. All must be working together in the manner intended. This would give consistent example and people would be able to accurately view the different strains of spirituality and identify that which is most pleasing to them.

My gaze was directed to the boundary in another area altogether. I saw yet another group of Dominican sisters. These had the same rhythm apparent, meaning standing in a circle, hands busy with the daily work and then lifting it all up to the

Lord each evening in unity. I noticed that they were definitively on this side of the line meaning they served from within the Church's teaching and tradition. And yet there was something notable and that was that their imprint was visible on the other side of the line. I pondered this for a moment, waiting for illumination and I understood in an instant that these sisters served non-believers or non-Christian peoples.

Jesus was alert as I studied this, infusing information into my soul. I saw that Jesus wanted their hands or daily work to be exactly as it was and their prayer life and faith practices to be exactly this way. This is subtle but the Lord is quite serious about it. He wants us, who serve those of different beliefs to be immovable about our own spiritual disciplines and traditions. We will help nobody by becoming lax in our practices.

People served by Catholic organizations need service, yes, but the Lord's goals will only be met if those served can also observe our commitment to our practices.

We serve as Catholics, deeply, deeply rooted in our beliefs and practices. Only in this way will the Lord's full plan be realized in every area we serve. Is it possible that if people have the opportunity to observe how Christians live they will be less shocked upon their death? It will be a more gentle arrival in the heavenly kingdom if one has had a glimpse of the manner in which the heavenly kingdom pulses. There is something very big about rhythm and movement. God likes it to be predictable and ongoing with fewer rises and falls, more soothing and expected practices. I think we are safer in rhythmic existence. People need to know that tomorrow will resemble today in order for their hearts to relax enough to grow into their spirituality. This is not always perfectly possible but some things can remain the same, such as prayer disciplines.

I saw that this particular project, which represented all of the projects like it, meaning those which included Catholic organizations serving God's non-Catholic children practically, had to be aware that fully half of their goal, in God's plan, was to illustrate how Catholics serve each other, working together, for a common goal. In the event an order or organization is removed from a given geographical or demographical project, as in closing down a service because of lack of manpower or funding, for example, those being removed should understand that the imprint and example of their work remains, in some fashion, in the area and on the people affected.

Given this image, it would seem imperative that we consider not only what we do, but how we do it. The living example of our Christianity is as important as the works of mercy to which we are brought by Christianity.

One more word on the efforts of ecumenism is as follows: when I saw those fashioning the ornamental items to be showcased for other Christian denominations, I saw another group working in the name of ecumenism. They were throwing rocks at other denominations. The ones being hit by these rocks were being hurt, quietly, and, saying nothing, simply turned away. I understood that there was a way of teaching the truth which was like taking a paper that had true words on it, wrapping it around a rock and throwing at someone.

Are you giving others the truth? Yes. Are you giving it with love? Perhaps not. This is a lesson for all of us, within the Church but also within our secular communities. We must learn to be gentle. It is very difficult for an individual to accept the truth when someone hurls it at them in a way which leaves a wound. We have all experienced this and this causes damage and pain which can reduce the positive effect of the truth and create resistance to accepting the truth. May the Lord protect His interests.

November 21, 2011

Today I came into the yard and listened to the sounds and noises of the workers. It was all reassuring and beautiful. My attention was immediately drawn to a group of men over by the side of the Church building, the same side where I saw broken windows in a prior vision, as well as hooligans throwing stones through those windows. These men were studying one of the large windows in the roof of the structure which was filthy and had been shattered, with countless rocks and projectiles thrown at it by angry mobs. It was daylight now, the morning after, let us say, and in the clean light of day all that remained was the mess. These men had only now arrived on the scene. Two studied the situation, discussing how to best replace the window.

I looked and saw that it had all now been removed, the shards and pieces, so at least now we had a clean empty space. As two of the men discussed what should be done, one man, a bit unlikely in that he was a new arrival to the holiness game, studied the situation. I looked at him and could see that he had the vision. He remained quiet but he seemed to know what to do.

He finally turned and received a piece of glass from someone behind him. He began to climb a ladder to replace the glass. He was supported on each side by the two men alongside him. He had designed the glass to slide right in and the place had been prepared perfectly so it was a snug fit. He did this methodically and confidently.

I watched all this with great interest, because I, more than he, understood what was at stake.

When the glass was fitted, it replaced something terrible. It would remain transparent because it was designed with a new material which would withstand any onslaught, anything slimy or bad. The sun would always be able to shine through unimpeded and I looked inside the Church and saw that an area of light would be available in the Church for the duration of time because of the quality and design of this particular window, its placement, its design and its make-up, those components of which it has been formed. The make-up of the substance was huge and I cannot find the words. It is something about the people involved and Vatican II teaching about the laity and clergy together.

I noted that these three men were not clergy but married lay men.

I was standing off to the side in the beginning of this when the men were consulting with each other about the project and one of them saw me watching with terrific interest and scrupulous attention and he met my eyes for an instant and smiled.

I was consoled because this reassurance told me that they would get it right, according to God's plan, and that my efforts at teaching were bearing fruit and that my suffering was being used. It would be a sad thing to have a project come this far and go badly and this was my concern as I watched them.

It made me think that there are people who can be trusted.

The Undefended Life

September 20, 2011

Today Jesus asked me into contemplative prayer. This is what I saw.

Jesus was standing on a beach. The wind was blowing and He raised His hands out and turned His face to heaven, absorbing the wind. He was praising the Father. He was exulting in the power of God as it blew through Him and into Him. Well, this began a whole study, much of which I will keep in my soul.

I understood so much in the image, even though I did not study Jesus as God. More, I rejoiced in Jesus as a man standing on earth but also completely glorifying the Father by His recognition of Him as Creator. I knew that all movement and motion is a gift of the Father only possible because God allows it. I knew that there was a difference in the movement and motion in heaven and on earth. On earth, man often moves from human instincts. These movements may not be in the divine will as in movement that we think of as criminal or immoral, ways we use our body that do not give glory to God. But Jesus, or any one of us, raising hands to heaven in rejoicing and asking the Father for a benediction on all humanity is using his body in the divine will.

In heaven, all movement is in the divine will and each person is completely united to and moving within the divine will. God allows perfect freedom and there is perfect safety for all. Also, of course, we are using 100% of our intellect, but we are not limited by our intellect as we knew it on earth. Sometimes explaining things can be tedious but if we understand that we are unlimited in heaven in terms of learning potential, we will rejoice in all that we have to learn.

Jesus said, ***"Do it with me Me, Anne."*** Suddenly, I saw that it was me on the beach raising my hands to the Father in praise. And I felt the joy of it and I certainly was drawn back into moments in my life where I felt the freedom and exuberance of such prayer. Jesus said, ***"Please do not live a defended life, Anne. I will defend you. Live in freedom and joy, praising the Father and celebrating My life because only in doing so will others understand Me through you."***

Jesus directed my gaze to others on earth who were living what He would refer to as a defended life. It was not good. They will never be done defending and they will never feel safe, either. They are seeking constant justification of their actions, many of which should not be defended but regretted. We must not defend that which we should have avoided. We should admit our faults and mistakes, apologize for hurt and get on with praising God, thereby teaching others to rejoice in the Creator in advance of heaven. Jesus wants us to live in freedom and then we will be modeling this for others.

We must think of ourselves as small lamps which give steady light. The base of the lamp is our humanity. People sometimes deface the base and scrawl graffiti on the base in an attempt to discredit the light which comes from God. Well, the light is the light and if it is pure light which does not distract people, but allows them to see more clearly the work that they need to do in their own souls then all is well. That must be our test. If we are enjoying praise and public acknowledgement, then we must be careful indeed.

Ultimately, people should not even think about the lamp in the room. They should simply get on with their work, taking the light source for granted. The people staring at the lamp do not understand the nature or source of the light or even that the lamp only gives light because it is plugged in. They want to unplug it I suppose, so they can deem it useless and be justified with their mistakes defended.

This was the experience of Jesus as a man and we must expect some of this experience in our own life.

September 26, 2011

The defended life is limiting for Jesus in this way. If we are defended and our existence on earth is geared to defending ourselves and protecting a faulty concept, such as blamelessness or perfect innocence, then we are not fully open to either God's grace or the love that He wants to fill our souls with for ourselves and for others.

Our eyes must be upward, to the heavens, much like a person who is afraid of heights but must cross a bridge constructed of rope. Never mind that the bridge has been built by the finest craftsmen of the sturdiest materials. The moment the wind hits the bridge and it begins to sway, the one making the crossing is tempted immediately to look down into the ravine and consider the carnage that will result if he falls.

This is temptation. We all suffer from this. The problem for Jesus is that we do not identify properly what the fall would mean or what the carnage would bring. More on that later. Living an Undefended Life would help us to say, "If I fall, then I fall. People do fall and I may be one of them. I will trust Jesus to be with me when I fall and I will try to cross this bridge because God is beckoning me to cross this bridge."

Keep moving, apostles. The Lord has the right to change the landscape as we walk through our life but we must keep moving toward Him. How many times have we experienced a bridge that is swaying in high winds? Sometimes we feel we are clutching the rope handles in terror with all thought of crossing gone. We are paralyzed with fear and yet there is the Lord on the other side with His arms open for us.

Pope Benedict XVI told the young people at World Youth Day 2011, "Do not let adversity paralyze you." This is a good warning for all of us. Life will always be changing, even when we are confined to a sick bed within the same four walls for days, weeks or months on end. What is in motion during that time? So much! We are becoming more detached from the world. We are becoming more aware of our powerlessness. Do the branches of a tree move because they want to? No. God allows the tree to move through the power of the wind. We must be assured that if God decides that the tree should remain still He will abduct the wind for as long as He decrees the stillness. So, too, each of us is able to move, physically, spiritually, mystically and emotionally because God wills the movement. We, with the free will we have been given, choose how to move in a given moment and in a given set of circumstances. God hopes that we will move in the rhythm of the divine will. God hopes that we will move to the beat of His Sacred Heart. He, after giving us free will, reverently respects our right to use this gift as we will.

The Undefended Life is one where we move freely, to the rhythm of the divine will, inhaling and exhaling the perfumed love that comes from the Sacred Heart. We assume the stance of Jesus on the beach; arms open and out, feet firmly planted, eyes to heaven, supplication to the Father coming from our lips. The winds of the world blow at us. We receive the wind, all coming from the hand of God, and return a continual stream of supplication. "Please, Father, bless mankind. Please, Father, let your will be done on earth. Please, Father, let me serve you in joy and trust."

This is what God has arranged for us. Jesus, on earth as a man, prayed, "Our Father who art in heaven." When He said 'Our', He identified the collective nature of all men and thus the collective importance of all men. We are all children of God as He was a Child of God.

"Who art in heaven…" God, while with us, is also removed from us in terms of our senses but Jesus puts God somewhere for us. He puts God in the Invisible Reality. God is real and He is in heaven.

Do not be afraid. He has not abandoned us.

"…hallowed be Thy name." Jesus shows us how to give God praise and bless His name and teaches us that it is important to do so as by reverencing His name, we also, albeit unwittingly, claim the dignity of being a child of this holy and sacred God for us and for all men.

"Thy kingdom come on earth as it is in heaven." By saying this we ask that we play our part in His will. We put our desires and cravings into the heart of the Trinity. We, too, wish this, Father. We want what Your heart desires, that on earth we will treat each other with the same dignity we are assigning to You and with the same dignity that the saints give to each other in heaven. Give us the grace to draw that desire into our day and make it happen around us though Your power and our willingness. Help us to live like saints in advance of heaven. This is possible and achievable with a very small bit of desire and willingness and copious amounts of grace, which God has for us and pleads with us, through Jesus, to accept.

"Give us this day our daily bread." Jesus, through this You teach us to rely on the Father for everything but also to accept what we have and thank God for it, not measuring our wealth in terms of that which is constructed by the world but by that which is offered from heaven, that is, goodness, kindness, holiness and an upright life, whatever the circumstances.

"And forgive us our trespasses as we forgive those who trespass against us." Jesus tells us, in summary, 'Go to the Father in confidence, acknowledging your humanity and your failures.' Failure and humanity are two very important words to anyone following Jesus because these words address both the first part and the second part of this line of the Our Father. We have failed through our humanity and others have failed us in their humanity. This, all by itself, provides a template for walking through life with gentle eyes on ourselves and others. The fact that the word 'trespass' is in the present tense tells us that others are not finished trespassing against us. Until our death, we will most likely be trespassed against. We must see this coming and not take it very personally. We must always be on guard that we not become a trespasser ourselves because that is the thing that we can control.

"And lead us not into temptation but deliver us from evil." Dear friends, this line reminds us that we must work for holiness. Jesus, in part, is teaching us to ask the Father for the grace to be spared avoidable temptations. As Catholics, we look on the Catechism as a roadmap to steer us away from dangerous temptations and to steer us into a life that is morally as safe as it can be. Jesus acknowledged the presence of danger in our world, that is, the oppositional force against which we toil, for ourselves and others. This line by Jesus prompts us to preach the Good News with determination. Deliver us from evil, us meaning the whole of humanity. What is our role in helping God to deliver humanity from evil? We must all decide for ourselves. Preparing children as parents, fathering souls as priests, giving Jesus our maternity for His desires as religious sisters, consecrating our single life to the Church for her goals of feeding the poor, nursing the sick and spreading the love of the Gospel message. In each commitment to every vocation, God has hopes that we will help Him to "deliver us from evil."

September 27, 2011

It is important to view the 'us' as mankind collectively and accept our responsibility as apostles to put our oar in the water of the boat that is the Church and begin to row along and help her to move forward.

If even a small portion of Christians tried to fully embrace their commitment to the Father's cause through Jesus, we would see a surge of wellness come into the world. Love is contagious, after all, and one Undefended Life which returns love for hostility can infect countless others because of the ripple effect. Our humanity seems repulsed at this when we begin but it is true that our humanity actually craves the freedom to relax into the human experience and praise God while also accepting and distributing His love. This is where we get the prayer coming from the whole heart which says, "Thy will be done." Many saying that prayer understand that they are agreeing to accept suffering and human hardship. Many wince even as they offer this congenial agreement to the plan of heaven because they know suffering will come and they also know that as Jesus accepted suffering, so must they. And yet, the Father is so pleased by the offering even though there is the wincing that comes with it. The Father says, "Truly this man loves because only love would willingly accept suffering for itself so that another's needs could be furthered."

This is what Jesus did as a man.

We are writing about the experience of Jesus as a man living on earth in a continual stance of praise, offering and supplication. We must see that we are in Christ and Christ is in us and together we live for the Father through the knowing that is the Spirit. This knowing gives us direction and hopefully constancy, once we are experienced enough to remain on course regardless of the temptations and distractions. Yes, the Spirit guides, but we must aim to supply the constancy.

We must examine constancy given that it is so important to the coming of the Kingdom. What is distracting to us?

Fear, clearly, as when the high winds come we all tend to seize up and hold our breath, even in our prayer lives. Hmm. We are all wondering what to do about that given that when real danger is present, we cannot help being afraid. If the bridge is swaying and the rope looks frayed, we are facing a fall, it is true. I suppose the best advice is to consider the Passion, examine the worst possible outcome and then rest in that possibility with Christ and picture ourselves dealing with that circumstance or circumstances with Jesus as a saint would. We should pick our favorite saint and wonder how this saint would navigate the circumstance of this particular bridge collapsing and hurtling one down into a ravine?

The details are different for every person's crisis, of course. A man once faced prison and said, "This I cannot do. I cannot and will not go to prison". The implied course, if prison became the outcome, was to him suicide, of course, because he was not a 'flee the country' kind of felon. He was sentenced to prison. He did go to prison, and he is not only coping but learning many sublime lessons about Jesus through his experience of Jesus on earth as a prisoner. Beautiful. The bridge he constructed in his head collapsed and he and Jesus together, fell into the ravine only to find that together, they not only survived but flourished spiritually.

We are all in prisons, my friends, all different but many the same. The dankest prison is that of being a prisoner to the opinions of others. This is probably the most common and most stunting in terms of the growth of the Kingdom coming on earth.

Jesus did not stand on the beach and wonder what others were thinking about Him. He knew they were not only thinking about Him but talking about Him and, what's more, some people were condemning Him. Sometimes people misunderstand us and move toward understanding and sometimes people misunderstand us and move toward condemnation. Should we change our undefended stance? Should we stop praising God so that we can turn our hopes and prayers to the human being who is making us fearful? Should we stop praising God and instead beg Him to make others like us? Where will this get the Kingdom? What will be the result of our distracted service? I will tell you. The result will be a sagging effort, an interrupted and disjointed flow coming through us because we are neither fully receptive to God's love nor fully expressive of God's love if we are not focused on the Father's approval but on man's approval. This is true and let us each listen carefully here. We have been placed in this time to serve. God needs to get the most out of us because many are not serving. If we offer a half-hearted effort others will not be loved or blessed and the whole campaign will be bogged down like a tank in the mud. What good is a state-of-the-art tank if it is stuck in the mud and cannot make it to the front line of the battle?

Apostles, this is what we resemble if we are catechized and blessed apostles who have been given contemporary and dynamic blessings for this time and we do not move into the battle. Worrying about the opinions of others is the mud in which we become mired. The result is that those working in the, it must be said, fierce battle of this time are working without the proper support. This is why so many apostles become tired and discouraged. The fellowship willed for them is languishing in the mud, with their state-of-the-art graces largely under-utilized. They are like children playing with steering wheels but never actually driving the car. The wheel of a car is meant for steering a moving vehicle. If we take all that God gives us in terms of these messages and blessings and fail to serve Him to the fullest possible extent, then we may be treating the battle of good versus evil as a spectator sport.

Dear apostles, what could be worse on the last day than having to look on that as our return on God's sublime gifts for this time in history? If mankind is in a serious time of decision, then let it be said that we are also being blessed with a serious amount of grace to not only deal with this time but flourish in this time and help all others around us to also flourish.

September 27, 2011

Undefended lives will create conditions for the greatest amount of love and grace to flow into the world. One by one, apostles will turn their eyes away from worldly fears and apprehensions and turn their eyes toward heavenly realities, unseen but readily identifiable in each day of every apostle's life.

Instinctive actions to defend our physical person are natural and built in to our physical organism. Into our psyche, too, there are instinctive prompts to defend ourselves from manipulation and abuse. We can become better and better at identifying threats to our psyche and understanding our emotional wounds. This self-knowing is a process which we are each called to begin at some time in our life. It is both our obligation and our responsibility. By examining and acknowledging our own wounds, we become less likely to act from them or indeed inflict similar wounds on those around us. We want to be healed and Jesus wants this, too, and it seems clear that Jesus is willing to be intimately involved in our very personal hurts and traumas by the specific words He has allowed from heaven in this time in the form of the "Heaven Speaks" booklets. Jesus, Himself, is acknowledging the very individual nature of our hurting and thus, because we seek to emulate Christ, we must do the same for others. It is too simplistic to look at others and point out their human failures without attaching those failures to wounds and comparing them to our own wounds and consequent failures, thus treating them with the patience and kindness that Jesus modelled during His life on earth.

Jesus did not take the sins of others and use them to shine a light on His perfection. But sometimes we can be tempted to take the sins or flaws of others and try to use that humanity to distract others and perhaps ourselves from our failings. We aim to use a lowered bar to measure ourselves. How many times have apostles come to me and said, "At least I am working on my holiness. I'm doing better than most people." This statement comes in many variations but it is always an attempt to 'compare down' if you will as opposed to comparing to Jesus Christ and how He lived His life on earth, a man, suffering and enduring and giving glory to the

Father in the most intimate and sublime relationship of mutual respect and commitment which ever existed.

Dear apostles, do we want this holiness? Do we desire to see what it looks like in ourselves? Then we must protect our stance of praising the Father from Christ in us. We must work from Jesus always. Jesus in us wants to view life a certain way. Jesus in us wants to view those closest to us in a certain way. Jesus in us wants to draw us into Him in a union that protects both us and the will of the Father. Jesus knows that if He can prompt us to rest in His presence in our soul, we will be calmed and comforted enough to begin learning about the stance of praising the Father. This 'working from the Savior within' will take us into the Undefended Life that God wills for us.

It seems that Jesus is drawing us into the very Trinity Itself. This is His goal. We become welcome in the living, pulsing love and reciprocity always moving between the Father and the Son through the Holy Spirit. We, in our humanity, can enter into this relationship through the humanity of Jesus Christ. That was the plan, it would seem, when God sent His only Son. This is what will occur when we are drawn into heaven. We will exist in union with Christ adoring the Father. Again we are looking at a foretaste of eternity when we look at serving from Christ to the Father through the Spirit. Jesus urges us to live like He lived, always in union with the divine will. This concept is perfect truth but elusive in its very simplicity. There are layers which must be explored for each apostle to grasp this truth in contemplation of the unique nature of Christ within.

September 27, 2011

Jesus Christ encapsulated all mankind, meaning, lest anyone wriggle from the proposed heavenly goal for his own nature, each of us was embodied in Christ's body as a hope of the Father's that we would, on earth, emulate the Son and be obedient to the divine will as the Son was obedient to the divine will.

Consider, for example, the elements of the Passion. The Undefended Life is never more apparent than when Jesus is the victim of the smear campaign by those who were envious of the effect His preaching was having on people. The Pharisees were heavily invested in the deference they received from the people. Jesus usurped their position, as they saw it, because He drew the eyes of the people to reverence which did not stop at any man but flowed naturally upward to the Father. The Pharisees wanted this reverence for themselves. They, in their attachment to their position, blocked God from the people. They were not permeable meaning, they claimed the goodness of God for themselves instead of inhaling love from God and exhaling it to the people as God's grace. Which one of us inhales oxygen and then claims the carbon dioxide we exhale? Isn't it true that we are all created equally in the right to inhale oxygen and then exhale it as something else when we are finished with it?

My friends, it is the same for prayer and grace. We inhale heaven through prayer. What comes from us, if we are actually inhaling it, are things like good works, charity, kindness and patience. All of the virtues emit from our Spirits because our soul naturally turns the prayer into grace. Now this is changeable in terms of what we can actually produce for humanity on any given day. Sometimes we gulp prayer like drowning men and do not see any return. Indeed, sometimes we are afraid we are a hazard to God and no matter how much we pray we do not experience consolation in the form of an orderly Spirit. That stated, we are being oxygenated through the prayer and God is storing it up through our suffering and through the withholding of consolation so that when someone is in need, our consolation will flow out and into the soul like water from a tap that is on full blast. The recipient does not know where the graces were obtained. The recipient only knows that God is generous in the extreme.

What about us, apostles of the Returning King? What do we gain? We gain a portion of the dignity of Christ because we have cooperated and indeed participated in the Father's Kingdom coming. What kind of sublime privilege is this that the Father allows this participation from His children? It is the privilege of embodiment in the King's human experience and human assignment, helping to make His Father's Kingdom come.

Look at the experience of Jesus falling while carrying the cross. Would there have been a temptation to remain down? Have we not all felt at times that if we stopped, then at least the suffering would be finished?

Every human being will at some time feel like Christ, crumpled on the ground under a heavy cross of suffering. As Jesus lay there surrounded by the force of Satan's hatred, it must be true that His humanity urged Him, 'Stay down. Quit. You have failed. They hate you and you are not helping the Father but insulting Him with your failure.' My friends, what extraordinary discipline to rise and finish the job, understanding that if this plan had come from the humanity of Christ, He would have had authority and right to amend it. But if, on the other hand, the plan came from the Father, He had an obligation to continue into it until either He completely ran out of strength or He died. He certainly must have believed that He had run out of strength. He had fallen. He was down, on the ground and for at least a time, paralyzed by exhaustion and the force of hatred directed at Him. His cup must have seemed to have at last emptied, in terms of what He could physically, mentally and emotionally handle. I do not say spiritually because Jesus Christ, regardless of His perception that the Father had either abandoned Him or was in the process of abandoning Him, was never detached from the Father through sin. So spiritually, Jesus was never unplugged. And that is probably what separates Him from each one of us, His servants. The symmetry of the Blameless One absorbing all of our blame is so perfectly masculine in that it points to the highest Fatherly protection of God's children.

The beauty of Mary, nurturing the Condemned until death

while risking her own life, similarly points to the highest motherly protection of God's children.

Who is like these two? To what can we compare their offering which is complete and moved them to the final limit of existence on earth, in other words, to the death and right into death itself where Jesus was concerned?

Jesus assumed the hardship of the Crucifixion. This would not have been asked of Mary in that way because Jesus, as God and in union with the Father, is the only One capable of such an action against sin. For Mary was reserved the more sublime suffering, that of the 'witness to the anguish'. She would have preferred to suffer it rather than have her Son suffer it. The Father watching Mary suffer this for the divine will reserved for Mary every possible intercessory power for His children because she proved herself faithful to the end to all of God's children, embodied in Christ Jesus as we are. To be clear then, she was not only faithful to Jesus, but to God, through the power of the Spirit and by this action she made an eternal act of fidelity to all of God's children. Mary would not claim anything. She would give credit for her perseverance to the gracious but forceful presence of the Spirit in her soul which propelled her both into and through Good Friday and upheld her until Christ revealed Himself to her in His resurrected self.

Mary is not God. She is not divine. She is a perfectly formed and preserved child of God. She, as first tabernacle of Jesus, also became a mystical tabernacle for humanity. She holds us all in her heart but Mary, as a created being, was not always and this differentiates her from the Trinity, who always was.

Mary would say there are many ways in which she is different but to go there would mean to leave the point which is living Christ's humanity in each day we spend on earth. St. Paul said it is not I who live but Christ who lives in me (Galatians 2:20). It is to be this way for all of us and Mary wants to mother us as she mothered Jesus unto death and that means to constantly support us in doing the Father's will. When we fall, she will draw us up and back into the existence of our passions. This is why the plan for Mary is so important in this time. Humanity is staggering and in some cases, humanity is down in terms of the goals of the divine will. Mary is waiting to help us up, to draw us along the path of salvation and safety.

She would say, "Move quickly now, into God's work."

October 3, 2011

As apostles, we strive to work from Christ in us, like St. Paul. Mary will help us to do this and Mary spent her life helping to look after God's will by helping to facilitate God's plan in others. Dear apostles, when we look at those around us, we must see a perfect plan in each person. God has willed that everyone we look at should live in this time. There is a purpose for each life. Therefore, if we are taking what is best about Mary's life, let us try to help facilitate God's plan in others. That means different things for different people and we view our vocation as a first stop to see what our role is in facilitating God's plan in those around us. As parents, we are forming. As priests, we are fathering. As sisters we are mothering. As religious we are living in accordance to the goals of our orders. As single apostles we are lifting up the Church in whatever way we can and are called.

Always, for all of us, we are called to facilitate God's plan in others by being a witness to faith. Others must look at us, praising God in all circumstances and claiming Him as our hope and our joy and they must then see a living example of how it is done. This, all alone, makes us like Mary. This, all alone, makes us like Jesus. And this, all alone, will bring others back to love.

When we admit that we are impoverished and that all that we possess, even our very matter, comes from the Father, we will begin to see that truly there must have been a plan for us because only God could take the opportunity of our parents' union and assemble the cells, organize them toward growth and send them into the world. We are a collection of living, moving cells. No more, no less, and yet, what comes from us is so impacting on those around us, also mere collections of cells. The Spirit, active in the soul of another, is impacted profoundly by our actions. Is this not true? Can we deny that our souls have been both blessed and traumatized by others? Would we say that the cells of our hands were affected by the cells in the hands of others? Barring physical contact, no. So then what is it? What is it that so exquisitely forms us? Is it the thoughts of another which prompt their words and actions that impacts us? But what are these thoughts? Where do they come from? More importantly, why does a man offer His life so that another man can live? Because He knows that the body is ultimately only a temporary collection of cells ignited by God and ordered to a higher plan. He knows that what remains after He is gone is an imprint to be claimed by the souls of others and He is trying to contribute a positive imprint for claiming by those who also seek to leave what is good and positive.

Dearest apostles, think carefully today. What imprint do we want to leave for others to claim and indeed for all humanity to claim? Remember that the whole world is affected by each one of us by virtue of the ripple effect. When we look back at humanity from the Invisible Reality after we are finished with our life, do we want to view others still suffering from the trauma of existing in our temporary presence or do we want to see others still benefiting from the blessing of our existing in our temporary presence? We all know dead people who hurt us. We strive to forgive them, of course, and understand their human frailties even as we take the best out of their examples. But their mistakes must prompt us to search for our mistakes and try to mitigate for our mistakes while we live. This is always possible, always, regardless of the extent of how we have hurt people. And please be assured, we have all done our share of hurting people so best if we get busy about forgiving others and forgiving ourselves and getting on with the healing which will bring us to offering the 'best version of ourselves', as Mathew Kelly urges.

Yes, the human body is a temporary dwelling place at best and we must bring the best out of our time in it, driving it gently but firmly into the divine will of each day. This is what Jesus did and this is what we must do.

Diocesan Priesthood as a Point of Entry for a Co-responsible Laity

Just as the cell is the first unit of life in the body, the person is the first unit of life in the Church. If the cells are not functioning properly or their environment is toxic, then the body will gradually weaken over time, and be at risk of death. In the same way, if individual Catholics are not functioning properly and their environment is toxic, then the Body of Christ is at risk of weakening and indeed, in some areas, of death.

We accept that a co-responsible laity is necessary for renewal to occur quickly in the Church. By Church, we reference primarily the international diocesan structure. We also accept that renewal must be an interior phenomenon, occurring in people more or less simultaneously in each diocese for the Lord's renewal goal to be achieved quickly. It is for this reason that the role of the diocesan priest is crucial in this time.

We consider that if the body is dehydrated, then it will not help much to rub water on the skin. It will be more efficacious to drink water and hydrate from the inside. And if the inside is dying for want of hydration, then the outside will not hold its look for long. Eventually, the signs of dehydration will appear to the outside world. If a body appears sickly and dry on the outside, that body inspires fear and uncertainty. If a body appears robust on the outside, that body inspires confidence in its wellness and abilities.

Point of Entry

The diocesan parish priest is the point of entry to the Church for the vast majority of Catholic lay people. It is he who opens the door to the Church and he who can also 'prop' it open so that even though people may walk past the door many times, when they see that it remains open they will, at some moment, obey the prompting of the Spirit and enter.

If the diocesan priest is discouraged, he risks projecting discouragement into his congregation. If the diocesan priest is cynical about the leadership in the Church, then, over and above the grave risk to the spirituality of the man, we have, heaven help us, an entry point attracting and forming exactly what we do not need, that is, lay people coming in to service with a spirit of superiority over the rightful authority of the Church.

As each parish priest knows, there is a divide between worldly thinking and worldly affairs and the affairs of Christ, the King. And, while it is paramount that we attract, invite and receive lay people into service in the Church, we must also be cognizant of the great need to provide formation for them as they arrive. Because each committed servant of the Church has learned, sometimes painfully, that all does not move in the Church as it moves in the world, we recognize that progress can look different from inside the Church than from outside the Church. While at times, worldly strategies are helpful to the administration of the Church, at times worldly thinking is directly at odds with the necessary growth of the Church. Often, explanation is imprudent or impossible. How does one explain the movement of the Spirit in the leader who cannot reveal all that moves him to his decisions? And which formation director has not struggled to form an older candidate with fixed and rigid opinions?

Yes, at times, human opinions and ideas are at odds with the destination God wills. And what may look one way in a business corporation looks quite another in the Church. How extraordinary is the necessity for patience and humility in the diocesan priesthood and how necessary for the successful integration of lay people into the being and action of the Church. If those struggling to understand the suffering of the international Church compare her to a successful business corporation, then truly those people will move further and further away from understanding and fidelity. The diocesan priest, receiving lay people for co-responsible service, will have to model a fixed and intelligent spirit of obedience if we are to promote obedience and not rebellion. Only in this way have we a hope of achieving unity.

Do we need aggressive leaders? Or do we need holy, humble and selfless men and women, willing to suffer and lead simultaneously?

This need for suffering leadership has its roots all the way back to St. Peter. It was St. Peter, himself, who learned about the Way when he offered the 'great idea' of erecting tents on the site of the Transfiguration, even as Christ continued on through time to His Passion, death and resurrection. Peter saw another 'great idea' rejected when he, with understandable worldly logic, began to fight for Christ in the Garden of Gethsemane. But again, we witness the Lord advancing, not into Peter's plan, but into the Father's will.

Brothers and fathers of the Christian family, be alert to the times. Consider your own formation and what helped you to persevere to ordination and beyond. Begin at once to impart this same formation, in some fashion, to those in your parishes whom you identify as possessing leadership qualities. The substance of the Church is about to absorb a new wave of Gospel preachers. They are lay people. They will need preparation and while this preparation may not stop with the diocesan priest, it will often begin with the diocesan priest.

Fathers, be reverent about what you are teaching tomorrow's leaders. It is you, the priests of each diocese, who provide the vantage point for most Catholics. Do they view the Church from the high ground that is hope? Or are you subtly or directly communicating hopelessness? Oh, the anguish you will feel if you lead God's children to cynicism when the truth is that we are individually privileged to be part of the rich faith community that is the Catholic Church.

We, as citizens of heaven, must promote all that is dazzling about the Catholic Church. The presence of Christ in the Eucharist alone is enough to prompt rejoicing in each parishioner if they are given even a small understanding of the Mass. And understanding is the key because the reality in many countries is that people have somehow divested themselves in a very short time of the teachings of the Church. The priest must be careful to preach, teach and model in every utterance and activity of ministry. And if the parishioners are allowed to identify the normal pattern of suffering, then growth, in the Church, then those Catholics will have a proper context with which to evaluate the current experience of the Church in many regions. Indeed, renewal is advancing nicely. Clericalism has been successfully reduced in many areas through a better understanding of the role which should be played by both lay people and clergy.

Fathers of God's children in the diocesan priesthood, consider what it was that first delighted you about the Church. What is it that delights you now? We must always return to our original delight and rediscover it, because "he who climbs, never stops going from beginning to beginning through beginnings that have no end." (CCC 2015)

The diocesan priest, as a curious and holy disciple, will move the Church into renewal like nothing else.

Truly, though, like tired mothers, the diocesan priest often cannot afford to leave for a sabbatical and must recover 'on his feet' so to speak. But the need for continuous service is no obstacle to renewal of the heart. God sends compassion and grace. And if we return to and rediscover that which delights us in the tradition of those who went before us, we will represent God's truth accurately, with passionate joy and conviction. In this way, those lay people answering the call of co-responsibility will find in their parish priest an encouraging and warm welcome into dynamic, active service.

With regard to the inevitable ups and downs of each faith life? God factors into His goals the human experience of each man and just as John remained with Jesus and Mary at the foot of the Cross through love, we accept that remaining in service during discouragement might just be the most sublime act of love we will have the privilege to offer heaven. Relationship with Christ presupposes suffering. And what looks irrational from worldly eyes is called perseverance in the faith life. Yes, when all else falls away, love holds a position.

Alongside Mary, the Queen of the Church, the diocesan priest, like John, remains in place so that the Trinitarian existence can be continually offered to God's children.

Welcoming Home Those Returning to the Sacraments

It is true that many Catholics currently live away from the sacramental life of the Church. It is also true that shifts in the world have created economic realities which have resulted in a lack of security for many. For this reason, many people, finding themselves less distracted by materialism, have begun to make their way back into the more stable experiences of their childhood, part of which includes their faith experience.

While this is a good thing in terms of man's search for a deeper meaning, the diocesan/parish priest may be ministering to people who are both wounded from a toxic environment and suffering a certain grief at the loss of that which they had considered to be secure, that is, financial stability. With regard to the toxic environment, the parish priest must be aware that to assist those returning to the faith, he is often compelled to direct them to treatment for various types of human afflictions. This human development must be promoted as part of the spiritual journey and not distinct from it.

In other words, the person suffering from alcoholism will be thwarted in a true spiritual journey. The person addicted to pornography will be thwarted in a true spiritual journey. The person addicted to shopping or gambling will be thwarted in a true spiritual journey. Spiritual formation for these individuals will include identification of and possible treatment for these problems.

Possibly, in this time as never before, the parish priest must view himself as part of a multi-disciplinary team which might include mental health professionals or social workers who are sensitive to our spiritual and religious life. It has really always been this way. And the priest who identifies the resources around him will be best able to assist God's children who are returning to the faith in human distress. The spiritual journey for many must begin at interpersonal awareness and recovery. This process will be necessary to avoid a 'split' or superficial religiosity which can mask wounds, hurt others and actually prevent growth.

Assistance with Discernment

There can be an occurrence in the conversion of some which includes a fierce dedication to devotions and/or a single-minded following of a given stream of spirituality in the Church. People can become so involved in a limited identity that they pursue it to the exclusion of their personal development. Families may watch with amazement and dismay as the newly converted one speaks of nothing else but their new interest.

This can be like romantic love in that it calms and hopefully merges into a committed relationship with the Church and broader Christian family. Or it can become something sinister which is a type of immature spiritual elitism having at its core a more defined relationship with the reality of darkness than the reality of salvation.

These groups must sometimes be thought of as cults. Truly, many Catholics seeking adjunct spiritual fellowship beyond the parish, wander into groups and find themselves drawn into sensational experiences. Fear can be used as a tool to attract people in that the leaders of some movements purport to know more about Satan than the diocesan priests who are the first fathers. Now, the average diocesan priest might be thinking, 'It's quite possible they know more about Satan than I. I give Satan little thought'. But Fathers know that children are best nourished by a staple diet of ordinary nutritious food. And the fruit of such movements is often not good. The movements inspire suspicion over rightful leadership and superiority over everyone who is not in the group. False prophecy may abound and serious interference with a person's freedom and intimate relationship with God can be evident. Many families have suffered greatly when one of their members becomes attached to certain groups.

Perhaps a good measurement could be applied by evaluating where the devotion takes the person. If it takes the person to personal transformation, that is a good sign. If it takes the person to enhanced commitment to vocation, then that is a good sign. If it takes the person deeper into the teachings of the Church, hopefully through a commitment to the parish, that is a good sign.

Conversely, if it takes the person to fear-based and rash decisions that go against the harmony of the person's loved ones and vocation, then there is cause for dismay.

Evaluation of a person's mystical experience is a delicate matter. Clearly, as spiritual father, the diocesan priest must be more afraid of doing violence to a person's budding spiritual contact than of debunking false mystical phenomena. And yet, how frustrating for a priest offering solid teaching to sometimes blank faces to see a parishioner rejoicing at reports of mysterious mystical phenomena in another location. This report by a member of one's congregation could be handled one of two ways.

The priest could, with great impatience, renounce the reported phenomena curtly. Many have and possibly from correct dispositions. Or, the priest could recognize in the report that the congregant is truly hungry for and searching for the profound. People are seekers and must be viewed as such. Clearly, fathers, some people will never find that which they seek because of instability. God allows for their progress to come in different ways.

We are going a long way around saying that if the fruits are benign or good, God's interests might be best served by the priest viewing the search itself as a good thing. If the fruits are suspect or dangerous, the priest has the obligation to direct away from a devotion or group for the people in his spiritual care even though he is risking possible upset and personal attack.

A few quick evaluative tools include: Is the person attached to a devotion or group speaking more about God's enemy than God? Is the group's spirituality fear based? Does it seek revolution against rightful authority? Is it inspiring superiority by claiming to be more 'in the know'? Does it inspire greater attachment to family, parish and diocese or less attachment to family, parish and diocese?

Try to view the faith experience of the person in front of you with exquisite reverence, even if it is clearly sensational and ridiculous. People cannot be directed into solid teaching unless they are met where they are standing. Spiritual maturity comes over time. Perhaps we view specific immaturity to mark where teaching is necessary in parishes.

For example, if there is a reported phenomenon which is clearly not supported by local authority, the priest can direct to an approved apparition which is supported. If it is prophecy which is terrifying to the person, perhaps the priest can direct into greater understanding of the role prophecy plays in both the Old Testament and the New Testament.

The mystery of our experience as spiritual beings is a reality for all of us. The diocesan priest must be thought of like a core priest, it is true, in that he is called to support the core teachings of our Church. And yet, we must never forget that the core teachings begin with mystery. All that is measurable must co-exist respectfully alongside all that is mysterious. And what can never be limited is the length God will go to in order to draw a person close to Himself.

As renewal takes place, people will be coming in the doors via different routes.

"I will say to the prisoners, 'Come out', to those who are in darkness, 'Show yourselves.' On every roadway they will graze, and each bare height shall be their pasture. They will never hunger or thirst, scorching wind and sun shall never plague them; for he who pities them will lead them and guide them to springs of water. I will make a highway of all the mountains and the high roads shall be banked up. Some are on their way from afar, others from the north and the west, others from the land of Sinim. Shout, you heavens; exult, you earth! (Isaiah 49:8-15).

In short, management of that which draws children back to God must be done delicately.

Isolation, Loneliness and Ongoing Transformation

All leaders experience isolation. The diocesan priest is called to be a leader for the Church on the local, parish level. The diocesan priest will, at times, experience feelings of isolation which are the inevitable by-product of holding a position of authority. Now, clearly abuse of power in the past by some has made the word authority a little frightening. Yet, authority must be held if we are to preserve the integrity of the sacraments. And the need to hold the position of authority in no way conflicts with the overriding obligation of the priest to allow God's love for His children a free flow through his priesthood. Any priest blocking this love or distorting it by abuse of power will be accountable. The question is how to find the balance, most particularly in a time when the priest is being called to cede a certain amount of leadership, if you will, to the laity.

Clearly, each priest will struggle with this himself and will find his holiness in this struggle because any authority assigned to us by God requires an individual to participate in on-going interpersonal development. This 'alone' work is everything. And while this feels further isolating, it is actually transformation. Who will deny that all real transformation takes place deeply inside and who more than a diocesan priest is called to ongoing interior growth and transformation? When a person is being studied as the diocesan priest/father is being studied by God's children, he must be as opaque as possible meaning people should see the man but experience Christ.

Oh, my. Such a burden. Such expectation. Fathers, realize that Christ wants to be Christ to His people and He is hoping you will allow Him. The difficulty comes when the man inadvertently takes ownership of that which Christ is doing because if we claim the success we must receive responsibility for that which appears to be failure from the eyes of the world. This would be hard to manage.

Our eyes must be eyes which rest on the Invisible Reality more than that which we can see. The parish priest is the ultimate seed sower. He watches as people move past him for a time in their lives. He, generally speaking, sows seeds which will be brought out in the future, in many different places in God's kingdom. Fathers, every Catholic remembers the parish priest of his child hood. The role of the man who first represented Jesus to us impacts in a way that should never be underestimated.

Does this prompt feelings of overwhelming responsibility or an understanding of the need for on-going contemplative prayer, personal development and continual adaptation to the needs of one's people? This question must be answered and the right answer must be that this should not be overwhelming to the man. And until the man can co-exist peacefully with both his humanity and the power of Christ in his priesthood, he has to be in a state of self-evaluation and search. And no doubt this is a moving target.

The diocesan priest is filling shoes for a time as part of a team of men who carry Christ sacramentally into families for the perpetuation of the faith. Indeed, we remember that the vocation of the priest is ordered to the holiness of the laity. So the priest is always studying his congregation to see best how to minister to them. The priest is selfless in his delivery of God's truth, overcoming his own trials in order to lead others through their trials.

All leaders are doing this, none more so than faith leaders around the world.

Which good leader feels like 'one of the men'? Well, all of them should in terms of recognition of his humanity but none in terms of constantly communicating doubts. The most effective leader will tackle his doubts and fears with a few trusted friends and through the overcoming of his human fears and conflicts, he will be the best person to promote confidence in God's providence. The most effective leaders hold a distance, not in their humanity, but in their presentation of their humanity. On any given day, the priest must reach back into heaven through his soul and grab what is holy to offer to the people. The beauty of God's presence and truth must be piped through the humanity of the priest like water through a faucet. And a well-constructed, challenging and honest support system is imperative for the man so that God can work with freedom in the vocation.

We stated that our humanity in no way deters God's kingdom from coming, but the humanity must be acknowledged, rejoiced in and ordered toward our vocation. Diocesan priests must submit to a spirituality which enables others to assist them interpersonally. This protects both the man and the people's experience of God. Therefore, it must be viewed as a grave danger when a man ordained to the priesthood consistently refuses to participate in the spiritual activities arranged for him by his Bishop. Anyone not alarmed by such rejection of Fatherhood, should be alarmed. And the priest is not his own priest, but the Church's priest and therefore, chain of command must generally be respected. The priest disrespecting the leadership in the Church is, quite possibly at risk of misrepresenting the Church to his people. Additionally, the diocesan priest does not serve at the behest of himself, but at the behest of the Bishop. Rebelliousness, as much as anything, is a sign of changing times because a house divided against itself will not stand and the priest who disrespects rightful leadership is holding a position of authority which, in a sense, he has forfeited by disconnecting it from its source.

Fathers, the times promise to become more uncertain, as opposed to less uncertain. Bishops make mistakes, it is true. So, also, do diocesan priests. Lay people sometimes have to watch with helplessness and alarm as a priest plays out his own issues from the pulpit. God's children would ask you not to do that. God's children crave solid and selfless leadership which does not confuse them. Each man ordained to the priesthood should do the hard work necessary so that he can produce leadership which is attached to the one true Church. At the very least, it is best if the man leading God's children in the priesthood wages his personal wars privately, against himself and his bishop if necessary for his conscience, protecting God's children from his process.

Now, it is true that God's children are interested in their parish priests. We want to hear about his struggles and need to know that he, too, struggles, but mostly we need to hear about how he overcame his struggles. Imagine how a populace would feel if in a time of national crisis the president came out and said, "It's a disaster. I cannot see any answer for our troubles. We are truly without hope." Fathers, this is not leadership. This is actually abuse of power because it is using power to do that which is the opposite of what authority should do and that is take responsibility for offering a Way.

We, in any form of leadership in the Church, must take responsibility for leading God's children into hope, regardless of the temporary appearance of external circumstances. When saints died for Christ they died in hope, not despair. And if the saints were led to a martyr's death proclaiming Christ and the hope of eternal salvation, how can we do less while we live? Will we allow the natural ebbs and flows of popularity to affect our certainty that we have been ransomed at great cost? No. Our kingdom, like Christ's, is not of this world and we must direct people continually into the hope that is heaven, which, we must remember, is real.

In times past, many children learned how to pray in their families. After this, they received tuition in prayer from religious sisters who taught in primary schools. The experience of children in the sacraments and the Mass punctuated what already existed, that is, a steady prayer life.

In this time, little such tuition exists for many children. There is often inconsistent prayer in the homes of Catholics and there are fewer religious sisters modeling holiness. True, for those families committed to their faith, there may be Catholic education which fosters a prayer life but even in these cases, there may be limited reinforcement at home. And many people who were formerly able to afford private Catholic schools are no longer able, distancing the whole family from the school as a source of catechism. And in some Catholic schools, ill-equipped or non-practicing teachers are actually doing more harm than good by misrepresenting the teachings.

The times, as always, have changed. The priest is no longer highlighting that which has already been taught. In many areas, the priest is providing the whole experience of faith formation. That means, Fathers, that education of the basic teachings must be facilitated through the touch points that are the sacraments. I am stating the obvious, of course, and no one knows better than today's diocesan priest. There can be frustration in parishes that people who do not practice take up a lot of resources through their desire to have children baptized, marriages blessed and dead buried in Christian burials.

Arguably, they could be turned away.

But they cannot be turned away. All must be facilitated as much as resources reasonably allow. These sacrament points are exquisite opportunities for Christ. The priest, while providing ministry to people who may be largely un-churched, is never more called to be a teacher. Basic teachings must be modeled first, through kindness and interest, and taught second, through verbal explanations of why it is we do what we are doing. A priest recently preached about cyberbullying, noting that the children/aggressors were not learning about 'Doing unto others' because nobody brought them to Church. In a landscape of consumerism crumbling, there will be broad despair and people who fifty years ago thanked God daily for their food, now feel deprived if they cannot eat the food they like at each meal.

Fathers, perhaps gratitude is the single missing ingredient. And when young people come into Mass and hear a priest talking about being grateful to God for food, education and parents, that child is possibly hearing something for the first time. Gratitude is not the prevailing practice in some cultures. But it must be for people to understand all that they have been given in a time when much of it is evaporating. If young Catholics can be made to lower their expectations for material wealth and greatly increase their understanding of their call to contribute, we will have vocations returning and we will have well-adjusted young adults.

Fathers, the Church is craving young women. Truly, she is aching for the feminine touch, which, in its own gentle way, points people to the service for which they are best suited. We have lopsided ministry without women. Each parish priest might draw young women into service by asking them to teach young children. This is an area where young women shine and if they are asked, Fathers, they will say yes. In this way, they will learn how to walk, so to speak, into ministry to God's children. And whether they marry or not, they will bring with them an understanding of what it is to catechize the little ones sent by the Creator. Additionally, their natural nurturing instincts will be allowed to germinate, reducing the horrible disconnect which allows abortion to be seen as an option to unexpected pregnancy.

This should be the greatest imperative in each parish. And, when young women serve, young men are inspired to serve, also. And we do not care which vocation a person chooses, as long as he or she views his or her life as ultimately being lived from a vocation.

We will not have renewal without young women, as well as young men, serving in each diocese.

There are difficulties for a parish priest in terms of logistics and also, it must be said, the over-hanging suspicion from the last period which required the most stringent self-examination by the Church. But this is no barrier. Indeed, the period itself brought about that which was necessary for the renewal in that it brought lay people into service more dynamically than in the past. And if a holy and mature woman could be identified to lead a team of young women into a program for enhancing catechesis of children, then this would be a wonderful start at recapturing the holy feminine influence in the lives of the children of the Catholic Church.

These points for consideration should engender an

examination of the role of the diocesan priest by all Catholics. If the Church is to truly absorb lay people in a way which draws more lay people and vocations, the diocesan priest will have to play a large role. Jesus Christ, the First Priest, has the plan to achieve each goal. He knows the regional issues. He has the power and He sends the holiness. But we have to be heavily committed to prayer in order to see the Way.

Contemplative prayer gently absorbs each individual into Christ where we can become what we are meant to become. Christ craves union with His priests, who are His beloved paternal army, fathering God's children on earth. A commitment by each priest to daily contemplative prayer will delight Christ. Also, Catholics, who, as we said are watching their priests, are never more edified as when they see their priest in prayer over and above the Mass. When a priest returns to the church for silent prayer with the people after a daily Mass, each person becomes reverent.

Fathers, give God's children the opportunity to see you in prayer and you will give them a great gift indeed. Also, they will all, instinctively, pray for you at those moments. Ask for prayer for your ministry and your intentions. People will respond. Catholics love to pray for their priests. And prayer unites like nothing else. Truly, when a priest asks his congregants for prayer he will receive it.

Men, especially, are moved by this because they share the struggle to conform to all that is holy and it is a powerful thing for a priest to ask for help from men.

And if there is a job to be done, then young men will be blessed by doing it. Young people, sometimes spinning in their search for identity, lock on to service as a stabilizer. Ask, Fathers. And if nobody responds, ask again. And again and again. Indeed, ask directly and compel people to say no to you if they will because at least they will know that they are deciding against service. This will decrease the comfort they might have in ambivalence as a way of life.

Everyone remembers a moment when he or she failed to do something he or she should have done. We must give young men and women this gift of regret, also, if they reject opportunity to serve. There is no time like the teen years for formation in service and we do not favor those we keep out of service.

Again, a committed lay person working as part of a team should be able to facilitate service for youth but the priest making the request will prompt the rightful feeling of obligation to the Church which can help counteract any post-Confirmation exit phenomena.

Fathers of God's children, a great renewal is taking place. Diocesan priests, as the first spiritual fathers of most Catholics, are called in a special way to be agents of this renewal for and with Christ. Their role, notwithstanding the suffering they have endured, is integral. Through contemplative prayer and a renewed commitment to discipleship, each diocesan priest will find the place where his vocation intersects with God's renewal.

The Resurrected Christ

The Resurrected Christ

If we desire a share in the divine life during our time on earth, we must be willing to allow the Resurrected Christ to live in us and through us. This will be accomplished through our willingness to stare into Easter Sunday joy, yes, and also Good Friday suffering and death. We will suffer, dear friends, during our time on earth and will offer our bodies to the Father at the end of our time, just as Jesus offered His body to the Father at the end of His life. Jesus died after fulfilling the promise of His life by death on the cross.

We can live, even during trials, the life of Christ. Let me explain. It is the same thing as saying the word 'HOPE'. Hope is the road on which we travel through suffering safely. Hope protects us from idleness in the spiritual life in that there is no greater call to do our spiritual work cheerfully than when we are suffering.

Being convicted about hope is the way we immunize ourselves from cynicism, which might be somewhere near the opposite of hope. When we sustain a series of sufferings, we can find that our hope is flat. We may kick it, metaphorically speaking, throw water on it, and even try to shock it electrically through our favorite Scripture or devotion and what occurs? Nothing. Hope does not leap. Hope sometimes lies still. This is a frightening state of affairs for those who are naturally buoyant. But humanity often only recognizes a suffering in another which he himself has suffered.

To examine hope that is accessible, let us look to Jesus on Easter Sunday morning. Imagine He is sitting outside of His tomb, which had enclosed His broken body, that is, the remnant of His expired humanity. Death had seemingly overcome Him. He was certainly not preaching with His mouth when He lay wrapped in burial cloths. No. There was no evidence of His divinity visible to human beings as the stone was rolled across the opening of the tomb. The crowds dispersed. For those who had been inspired to hope through the life of Christ, all hope would seem to have died. Imagine them walking away. Would it be accurate to say that their legs carried them away from the savagery of the Passion only through the action of the Spirit of hope remaining in them?

My friends, breathing itself illustrates some degree of hope. And it is for that reason, the absolute requirement of hope to keep a person inhaling oxygen and exhaling carbon dioxide, that Satan cannot extinguish hope in humanity. Only God, who breathed hope into humanity when He breathed life into him, can reach into our humanity through our souls and draw back life into Himself. When we take a life, through violence or euthanasia, we are trying to be God. We, through the very gift of our free will, given to us by the Creator, attempt to force God to submit to our will. How embarrassing is a belief that we hold anything near to the wisdom of the Creator! Abortion, euthanasia, and indeed any murder, makes us pitifully arrogant. We are pretending that we hold the wisdom to extinguish hope because when we extinguish life, we have decided that no hope should exist in the life God created. If life is cooperating with the oxygen God provided, there is hope. Period.

But hope is a funny thing. It is just like oxygen in that it is invisible. It is like the wind in that it can often only be recognized by its effects. A mother feeds a sick child. She has hope the child will be restored or she would stop feeding the child. A terminally ill patient is given water. Why? We have hope that the person will be sustained and comforted, but for what purpose? So that he can continue to inhale and exhale oxygen, thus, preserving hope for all of humanity until that person has completed his or her time in humanity. When, through God's decision, that person surrenders his body to the Creator and advances into timelessness, hope is not extinguished, it simply transfers into those who remain with even greater abundance. Who would deny that they feel the spirit and presence of their ancestors who have gone before them, if only for an instant? Hope is something like oxygen. We must be careful never to pollute it, deny it or damage it in another. And the Resurrected Christ lives in each one of us who welcome Him. We must never be more certain of this than when we are suffering desolation.

January 23, 2012

Let us imagine that when the Lord viewed His Passion and death from the place of His Resurrection, He saw that He had all He could manage on the cross in the physicality of His suffering. He, who possessed hope for all humanity, fought the greatest battle ever fought for hope. He did not die in desolation, despite the circumstances of His death. He died in hope because He retained His hope against the enemy's effort to destroy all hope for all time for all people. The Lord looked upon the physical reaction to the suffering, which, it must be said, took place not in one part of His body but in all parts of His body. He was wounded simultaneously and thus, as a human being, was trying to tend to Himself in that suffering in many, many areas, physically, emotionally, spiritually, psychologically...the Lord truly took it on in every area all at once.

We resemble Christ when this happens to us, that is, many sufferings at one time. One suffering can impact all of these areas and we will have to be busy tending to all of the areas during the time of the suffering and after.

What will we look like when we are suffering grave trials?

Well, did Christ look like a King when He trudged up the hill, bleeding, seemingly powerless, mocked and rejected? Did He look like a King when they took away even His clothing, rendering Him naked before cruelty? Did Christ look like a King when they nailed His beautiful hands and feet to wood, something the Father created in His great benevolence? The answer is no. And each one of us is a treasure, like Christ, in that we were created by the Father to be reverenced and assisted by others as we make our way through the sufferings in our lives.

Apostles, when people are suffering the many aching passions in their lives, they will show signs of wear and tear. Christ is the jewel of humanity. Christ is the only perfect specimen. But He did not look like that when they turned on Him, distorting his Kingship to the furthest possible extent by disempowering Him completely. What emerged from this situation?

The King emerged.

Untarnished. Undiminished. Undaunted. How did Jesus feel on

Easter Sunday? He felt like God. But He did not feel like that as He suffered on the cross.

The Resurrected Christ, this Jesus Christ who returned to life on Easter Sunday, wishes to live in us. In so far as we allow Him, He does so. When people around us are suffering, they will not necessarily feel the extent of either their beauty or their sanctity. It is we, the brothers and sisters who surround them, who must remind them that they are beautiful, that they are holy and that God is filled with hope about them. This applies to those who are suffering addictions, suffering marriage failures and family disunity, incarcerated in prison and those who are not feeling joy in their vocations.

Jesus was probably not smiling from the cross. Our own humanity will reflect our suffering as the Lord's humanity reflected His suffering. We must minister to others accordingly, with compassion, understanding and a great deal of tolerance at how their humanity recoils at the cross.

For ourselves, we must go to our safe place, our sanctuary, and, with all of the kindness and compassion of the Savior who also suffered humanity, we acknowledge "I was afraid, and then I did this. I was alone, and then I did this. I was hurt, and then I did this. I was addicted, and then I did this. I was in grief, and then I did this." This formula or method of examination will predispose us to mercy for ourselves and also understanding of others. We use the formula not to make excuses but to seek understanding of our very real human wounds which can prompt sinful actions.

Young people who come into the faith early and learn to self-examine properly are so very blessed. They begin the hard work of appropriate self-examination young and thus do not store it up for a big job later. If one is only beginning real self-examination at an old age, one may have an awful lot to examine. This method of 'doing the hard work in our heads' will leave us very free. Nobody will be able to convince us that we are without value. Additionally, nobody will be able to convince us that any created child of God is without value.

It must be so that Jesus, looking back at the figure of Himself on the cross from timelessness, felt reverence at the extent of His suffering, but also reverence at the extent of what was given to humanity through His suffering. Because He, as God, is aware of the gift given, redemption, He, Jesus, would do it all over again for each person if such a thing were necessary.

We must accept the reality of that gift now, in advance of our death, because if we do so then we will be living the Resurrected Christ. He will be living through us dynamically, impacting the world freely through our presence. This is what He wants for us and this is the plan for renewal. It takes study of both light and darkness in us. It takes willingness to transform. It takes determination, not to point at others but to be willing to examine ourselves.

In viewing the image of Christ resurrected, it is clear to me that when Jesus rose again, He had the ability to survey God's earth and creation in the calm wisdom of one who has triumphed over His humanity. The necessary period of temptation had passed. There was, indeed, the tableau of suffering and the great and terrible Passion, yes, but the Resurrected Christ was able to look deeply into that suffering and beyond it, around it, over it and beneath it, both in time, meaning at the other things that were occurring in the world in that moment in time, and out of time, meaning at all that would occur before and after that moment in time as a result of His willing acceptance of the cross.

The Lord, Resurrected, could see it all.

I saw the Lord, from the cross, look over at the suffering of an apostle years ahead into the future. The apostle crumpled to the ground in temptation to surrender to despair. As Jesus saw the apostle suffering, disheartened, and tempted to give up, Jesus called on the Father for strength and He felt fresh determination going into His body. Jesus then pushed strength out from Himself into the apostle in the future and said, "Go. Go. Continue on! Do not stop. Do not give up. All is courage. All is strength. The Father wills it, apostle. Go forward without delay."

I saw this apostle, begin to move again, first taking a few steps forward, then walking steadily, then moving with a determined, fast movement that allowed nobody to interfere. Nobody could keep up. They could not distract this apostle because the apostle never again took his eyes off the Father. To get to the Father, the apostle had to move further and further into His will and the apostle, once his gaze locked on the Father, never looked back again.

Oh, that this would describe us all and in truth, it does describe us at times. If we could see the Lord, in His anguish, willing strength into us through His torturous circumstances, we would have no fear of being overcome, regardless of what others did to our bodies or our reputations.

Christ on the cross saw everything, even while He was deprived of nearly all faith. The sneering of the tempter became, to Him, evidence of God's presence in His suffering, as opposed to the opposite. Jesus was determined to procure strength for us, those charged with pulling and carrying the Church into the future. And truly, as a Church, we, like Saint Paul, are straining forward. If we are not straining forward, dear friends, then we are drifting backward. Yesterday's graces are used up, like empty water bottles. People who carry them around, pretending to drink from them are also pretending to be hydrated. They are not hydrated. They are thirsting for the living water of God's presence in this time. Their sneering should be evidence to the new apostles that they are getting it right, not wrong.

The Pharisees did not to accept the Christ because acceptance of Christ would mean surrendering the place where they had ensconced themselves as kings. Pharisees will always reject the moving Spirit because they have set up a camp. They are complacent, immovable. So be it and may God protect His interests but let apostles of the Returning King be heartened by the truth that before the King departed from His earthly throne, the Cross, he pushed strength for this time into each one of us.

Meet His gaze, apostles and you will find courage. He secured everything that we would need for every trial. Be aware that when those who have set up camp are challenged to shift their positions, they can erupt in outrage and defend their 'kingdoms' with violence.

Today's apostle is committed, determined, willing to serve with his or her whole being and unwilling to slow down for anyone. Today's apostle has overcome His attachments to the degree that he has separated out his obligations from his distractions.

March 6, 2012

Today I watched as Jesus surveyed the world in His Resurrected body. He sat quietly. I sat beside Him against the stone wall and looked at His left hand. I was mesmerized because there was something different about it. Something about the same vibrations no longer necessary to hold the body together so the organs could function. The resurrected Jesus possessed stillness in body despite natural looking movements and total presence. His resurrected body was the same and yet different, making me wonder if this is how ours will be, also. I believe that I was distracted in this occupation, yet the Lord allowed it for a time. He then drew me into His study and I saw Him looking at the Passion again. I asked Him if He was looking at the Crucifixion and He said, *"No, I am looking at suffering and its impact."*

I understood that He was gazing at the thief crucified next to Him. This man appeared to die in a state of non-repentance. We have no way of knowing if that is true because he possibly lacked capacity for rational self-examination. We simply do not know. At any rate, I understood that he was guilty as charged. In a sense, the condemnation was righteous in that this thief had committed the crime he was accused of and sentenced according to the guidelines present at the time and in the place the crime was committed.

What is wrong with the situation?

According to the Lord's study, the treatment of the man, guilty as charged, was creating a greater trauma on the people in its cruelty than the trauma of the man's crime. Why? I understood that when people witness suffering they also suffer. Suffering moves out and this is consistent with the truth that the sin of one man first wounds him and then moves with great determination out into the world to do more damage. The hope is of course the opposite which is that virtue practiced by a man first blesses the man and then moves out with even greater determination into the world because it is carried on the wings of grace.

At any rate, people understand the man's sin and possibly that violence is a crime. It is much more wounding for them, though, to witness the collective hostility of a society when that society treats a man with total condemnation. This scene and my understanding of this scene casts a very serious light on any death penalties.

Jesus' view of this seems to be that the people are far more wounded, emotionally and spiritually, by the murder of the criminal or the mistreatment of the criminal than by the criminal's often irrational crimes. People can understand why a man explodes into criminal behavior. We have the human sciences now to help us even further to view criminals with compassion and understanding. God gave us these sciences to become more compassionate and to be also compassionate with ourselves.

But how then, does it add up, that we are still condemning men to death? I believe Jesus, through this vision, is telling us that it does not. Perhaps we should not be acting in such condemnation to people who, through invalid moral choices, commit grave crimes. I believe Jesus would say that many criminal choices are invalidated through serious limitations in mental or psychological health, often limitations which certain criminals have no choice in or control over.

For example, mercy would say that the addict chooses to pursue an addiction but that the addict does not choose the mental state which compels him or her to steal for drugs. That mental state is the result of the addiction, it is true, but is not the goal in pursuing the source of the addiction. The mental state is created by the body's violent demand for the substance. The culpability is likely reduced.

I see that the point of the vision is that when the collective society acts out violently, in the case of war, neglect of the elderly, failure to protect the unborn, and imposing a death penalty, we are all wounded. The result is that society begins to deteriorate into pain-led decisions in both personal and public life.

This is serious, indeed.

Thursday March 15, 2012

We consider the Lord on the cross. He gazes from His resurrected body at the time spent suffering while suspended above those living in the comparative safety of not being condemned at that moment. While each person viewing Jesus Crucified thanked God that he was not the one suffering, each person knew that the cruelty that pierced the hands and feet of Christ could swirl into a storm of condemnation and land next on him.

Such terror the Crucifixion imposed on those watching.

Jesus, suffering agony, must have craved reassurance and love. He must have craved validation from humanity. How He must have craved a voice telling Him that He was righteous, that His suffering was valid and valuable. What voice reached him? Whose voice could find Him, suspended as he was on His earthly throne of the cross? It was the voice of the good thief that sent words through the air into the humanity of the living victim. The good thief sent validation through his recognition that the Lord was innocent and thus, as completely innocent, a true victim.

There are many layers to a person suffering through time, meaning, living his life in exile on earth. The man trapped in his humanity for the purposes of his own redemption and the furtherance of God's kingdom receives the inevitable suffering in his mind, yes, but also in his heart. We can know that suffering will come to us and we can accept this suffering on behalf of the God who created us and the Son who redeemed us but our mind will have to work very hard indeed to steer into our innocence when we are innocent and steer out of the guilt others try to stamp onto our foreheads. This hard work of holding on to His innocence was no less for Christ. Indeed, so total was the Lord's condemnation, so irrational was the Lord's sentence that the mind of the man must have 'tripped' while trying to absorb it.

We can also 'trip' intellectually when trying to absorb irrational attacks of others. We are sometimes guilty, it is true, and self-examination reveals that we are not blameless, regardless of how poorly or clumsily others handle our imperfection. But sometimes we are innocent and that work will be very important indeed because by suffering as victims we are drawn into a scene that can resemble the Passion.

By witnessing others reject courage in favor of ambivalence and thus miss the opportunity to stand with us in righteousness, we can be drawn into disillusionment. Poor Jesus. How must He have felt about leadership as Pilate failed in courage and integrity? What was the wound when a man charged with protecting order stood back and allowed a mob, whipped into frenzied excitement, decide the fate of an innocent child of God? The disordered insistence of complete guilt alone should have alerted the leader that time was necessary to sift through the facts and allegations. But no. He stepped back. And Christ was delivered to the one who hates comfort and safety for all of God's children.

Yes, the wounds of Christ went far beyond the physical, deeply into His heart as God and as man. And it is this secret suffering that must surely have tempted Him the most, the temptation to disillusionment and despair. What is the point when good men will fail to stand for good? What is the point when leaders fail even one person through cowardice? Truly, these things must have tormented the son of Mary as He agonized through His last hours.

It must be stated, leaders are called to steer humanity toward God's will, not away from God's will. And as the bulk of humanity will recoil at the sacrifice necessary to be drawn toward God's will, the bulk of humanity will at times reject the messengers, the leaders. Leaders must contemplate the courage of Christ when He stood in for the Father till death because they, too, could be tapped for total integrity in the face of opposition.

We study once the again the relationship between Jesus and the good thief. The good thief must have railed against his sentence of death and the cruelty that meted it out to him. Yet through his sentence he was raised aloft with Christ and he was able to console Christ in a moment of exquisite temptation to despair. Would that each prisoner understand how uniquely placed he is to minister in the smallest of ways to those around him. Would that we, suffering from the place of our prisons of sickness and pain, understand how uniquely our crosses position us to help others suffering the same adversities. The beauty of the good thief shines out of scripture in flashing lights to those looking for validation, despite the inevitable guilt that comes to us from our fallen natures.

Apostles, we must work hard to comfort others, despite our condition of sinfulness. We must accelerate our daily ministries, in our homes and in the world, despite the realization of our sinfulness and failure.

Serve on, soldiers of the renewal. Do not be an obstacle to Christ. Truly, Jesus craves relationship with all and Jesus has never been more willing to accept the crumbs from the table of those who reject Him.

Citizens of Heaven

It is so easy to flee from the reality of obedience, contenting ourselves with fine theories about it. It is so easy to evade it, claiming the right to affirm our personality on the grounds, we say, that we have received it from the Lord. In reality, when we are honest with ourselves, we cannot but admit that obedience is not easy. There is a great risk of forgetting this... Left to ourselves, and living in the sight of God alone, His light should be our sole guide; but often, the absence of friendly feedback from our brothers or from those on whom we depend, leaves us drifting at the mercy of self-will, (Carthusian miscellany p. 187).

It would seem at this time in Church history that a great deal of confusion has descended upon many about the basic teachings of holiness. Obedience for example, has been vilified to the degree that one could become persuaded that obedience is in actual fact a rejection of one's personhood. How complex it is made to appear. How distorted a lens has been placed on the soul's need to conform to the civic responsibilities one is called to meet as 'citizens of heaven' (Philippians 3:20).

The difficulty with this is that without obedience we are driven through our lives like excited chickens, propelled hither and yon by self-will. Truthfully it is only in and through obedience that we can relax enough to actually discover our authentic personhood. And if we, as Christians, cling to the limited reality that is sin by teaching it to the exclusion of mercy, or, conversely, refusing to identify sin and ignoring it defiantly, or, again, minimizing its negative impact by claiming that it is inevitable, then God's children are missing their chance to change the world.

It appears that simple.

Perhaps we are in need of a collective reality check, a start over, a moratorium on focusing on the sins, particularly the sexual sins, of everyone else and issuing a call to virtue that does not BEGIN with sexual sin but advances in spite of its reality. Of course, not everyone is sinning sexually every day. But certain brothers and sisters are living lives that, while possibly very holy, are structured around a relationship that seems to include sexual sin. Many problems come from this but possibly not the problems people assume at first glance.

We, in this period of history, seem to have achieved a reality of sexual license and also an obsession with all things sexual. This has created a vacuum of expectation for many, meaning, for example, that if someone is living in an irregular union, we risk losing a potential unit of mission by casual rejection of the potential for holiness of those individuals. The truth is much deeper and the apparent surface sexual sin should not prevent anyone from having both hope and expectation of all Christians and specifically Catholics. I say apparent because, in truth, nobody knows what people are doing and usually the affairs of others are not our business.

Now the couple may say, 'Our sharing of sexuality is blessed because we love each other and we are in a committed monogamous relationship.' And yet our Catechism is telling us something different. Our Catechism is telling us that the sexual faculty is reserved for a man and a woman united in holy matrimony. And so we have an apparent impasse and some in the Church limit their view of the individuals to an immediate and total denial of the possibility for magnificent contribution and advancement into holiness in the couple involved in an irregular union.

Perhaps we might look for fruits. What are fruits of legitimate love? Sacrifice, one for the other, advancement in virtue, some contribution to the well-being of society in general? These would be good signs that something positive is happening between two people. Interpersonal flourishing and an increase of virtue should be seen. Because it is true that two people, moving through life, sometimes find one another and connect at a deep level. The connection is so true that the sexual expression is nearly incidental. It is surface, as it were, and the truth of the matter includes the depth of the interpersonal connection occurring between the two people.

By focusing on the possibility of on-going sin in the relationship, we are discounting an enormously important truth which is that the capacity for good exists between them and often they are acting as a balm and a strengthening agent to each other through their commitment and friendship.

'But people in irregular unions should not be marching up the aisle to receive Communion'. I've heard these things repeatedly and in very unkind ways. The truth is not the truth if the Spirit is wrong, of course. To clarify, though, the Catechism states, "According to the Church's command, after having attained the age of discretion, each of the faithful is bound by an obligation faithfully to confess serious sins at least once a year. Anyone who is aware of having committed a mortal sin must not receive Holy Communion, even if he experiences deep contrition, without having first received sacramental absolution, unless he has a grave reason for receiving Communion and there is no possibility of going to confession." (CCC 1457) So, to be accurate, no person should be receiving communion if he is in a state of serious sin. It is up to the individual and possibly the priest assisting them to determine who should and should not be receiving Holy Communion. And it is up to each individual to self-examine and determine what his role in the Church should be and to evaluate what his level of participation should look like in the Church. Clearly, God needs us all contributing.

For example, citizens of heaven have obligations and the Church, as the Body of Christ, has needs from everyone. So we must each ask ourselves what the Church is asking from each of us given the reality of our lives. If we are living in an irregular union and we feel called to remain with another person, and we are sinning sexually, and discussion with our priest confirms our condition, then we would presumably not receive Holy Communion out of respect for the teaching. My friends, we should remain in attendance at Mass and if we are lay apostles, at our weekly Holy Hour. We can make a spiritual communion when others are receiving Communion. Also, we will answer for our obligation to spread God's gospel message of mercy so we must be attentive to our Christian duties in our homes and in the world. God will hold us accountable for catechizing our children and keeping holy the Sabbath. There can be a temptation to throw out all of our obligations because we are temporarily not living one.

In our apostolate we commit to treating others with patience and kindness as seen by Christ in Holy Scripture. We also recite our pledge to God the Father offering Him our life, work and hearts. We are in a prayer group that meets once a month and we aim for monthly confession. Truly, this way of life is accessible to anyone seeking to receive Christ into His heart and offer Him to others. And we must assume that not everyone will be fully compliant at once. Maybe to begin, a person starts with the daily Allegiance Prayer. That, my friends, will give all of heaven joy, regardless of the rest of the circumstances around a person's life.

In the Lord's time, He saw that the Pharisees were focusing on the external performance of men, meaning the Pharisees were all about the law and how the law was being observed. Jesus treated this as a distortion because He knew that the purpose of the law was to lead people into and also protect a relationship with God. The law was there for the men. God did not create humanity for the law. The law was intended not to protect itself, but to protect man's ability to be involved in a loving relationship with our Father.

Moses in Deuteronomy 5:1-33 tries to persuade the people to accept this law saying that the law would make them wise and they would be able to be close to God. But the cultural development seen in the Lord's time was that only the prescriptions, 'the do's and don'ts,' as it were, had taken over. Many lost the plot.

Jesus in His Sermon on the Mount talks about anger in the heart and self-serving actions completed for attention and notice. This is another reference to the need to transform through the law and not follow the law while harboring all manner of bitterness in the heart.

And in the Gospel of Matthew 5:17-20 we hear that Jesus came not to abolish the law but to bring it to its completion by drawing man into the Lord's own relationship with His Father. Jesus spent time with people who were under the critical eye of the 'experts' such as the tax collectors. When he called on Levi, the man was delighted. The Lord had the ability to see past the law and focus on the heart and the performance of the heart compared to the actions which were disordered by impure motive.

In the Lord's time, we see hearts that were properly ordered but which were possessed by people who were falling down in places with regard to the 'do's and don'ts'. And we see people who were getting the law right but who were falling down in terms of what was coming from their hearts. So maybe the Lord wanted all of them to move into purity and maybe the Lord wants this now.

I am saying that if each man is examining himself, he will

determine where he has to move and with God's grace he will decide which area is possibly his Achilles heel. So if I am living according to the Catechism, then I must thank God that circumstances in my life are such that I am able to do so, emotionally, physically, psychologically and spiritually, meaning, I know what the Catechism teaches and why and all other things are equal for me.

I must then examine what is coming from my heart. It is the same as what was coming from the Lord's heart? Am I willing to be peaceful around 'tax collectors and sinners' with love and acceptance of the importance of what these others are offering and where they are outpacing me in holiness?

If, however, I am not living according to the prescription, the 'do's and don'ts', am I living according to the Spirit of the prescription, meaning, is what is coming from my heart consistent with what came from Christ's heart? Am I kind and loving, am I tolerant and accepting? Am I able to acknowledge that many of those living according to the prescription are sacrificing in order to do so and are accurately following the Savior of all mankind? Or do I resent their faithfulness and envy their compliance, viewing it with mockery and bitterness? Because if we are not in a position at this time to follow all of the 'do's and don'ts', that is one thing. We are accepted by Christ in love, no question. Christ sees each of us as a work in progress. But if we assume that everyone who has ordered his or her life to the 'do's and don'ts' is a closet Pharisee who judges all day long, then WE are getting it wrong and this is an attitude that is not in keeping with the people Jesus Christ was attracted to during His life.

Let us pretend that defiance, bitterness and envy are the same as having a high temperature. These things are symptoms, not of someone else's illness, but of our own. If my child is hot to the touch and I record an elevated temperature with a thermometer, I will not say, "My guess is that the neighbor's child is sick". I will say, "Clearly my child is sick".

My friends, if we are suffering with bitterness, defiance and envy, then we are very sad inside. God loves us all the way we are right now. We should not envy anyone.

Being in a relationship with Christ insures that the heart is ordered to love and then, what comes from the heart will also be ordered to love. If what is coming out from us is bitterness then what is inside the heart must be bitterness. We distinguish fleeting temptations from fixed, unexamined and complacent positions of being against any group rather than for God's kingdom coming on earth.

Indeed in the Gospel of Mark Chapter 7:14-16 we read that it is not what goes in the body that makes people impure but what comes out from the heart that is telling with regard to impurity.

With this stated, it must be recognized that if we are starting with the limited measurement that is the physical expression of sexuality, we will be handicapped in judging the condition, never mind the potential for holiness, of any individual.

To add the obvious, we should not put ourselves in the position of judging anyone but rather of loving everyone.

That stated, we know that truth is objective and that as Catholics we aim for compliance with the teachings of the Catechism. We should be careful to focus on our Vertical Relationship with Christ. Compassion for others should come from that relationship. We should never be lured into a mob mentality which excludes others from either worship within the Church or service to the Church alongside and indeed inside of our groups.

It must be true that each lover of Christ will have more in common than not in common with others, regardless of how people express their sexuality.

Remember that living sexuality properly supposes maturity. Living sexuality like a citizen of heaven supposes a very high level of self-mastery, indeed. A life of chastity, according to one's vocation, for many people, will be something that is acquired over a long time, through a very exacting process which seeks to absorb teaching as one is able. Additionally, there can be physiological realities that make self-mastery a longer process for some than others. And if we are honest with ourselves, many of us will admit that we did not or do not understand the fullness of the Church's teaching on sexuality. The truth is that most Catholics remain unenlightened and lack full understanding of the Catechism, which leaves them, therefore, unable to depart from the 'do's and don'ts' and land on the beauty of relationship.

Given our often limited humanity and given the reality that the current culture is over sexualized and distorted to an odd and an alarming degree, it might be best if we, as God's children, get on with the preaching of the Gospel from the starting point of love and potential for holiness, seeking inclusion rather than exclusion.

Additionally, it might be best if we start somewhere other than sex.

It is not going well, brothers and sisters, and partially this might be because all that anyone ever talks about is who is doing what with whom sexually while at the same time we have the dark underground circus of pornography luring even those who are full believers in the teachings and who are trying their best to be compliant. We clearly need God's help with our sexuality and it is time to be energized by beautiful Catholic teachings such as Theology of the Body, Natural Family Planning and Napro Technology.

Christ was a gatherer. In Matthew 12:30 Jesus says, ***"Whoever is not with me is against me, and whoever does not gather with me scatters."*** My dear friends, if we are overly insistent on a harsh view which focuses on the external performance then we, like the Pharisees, will be contributing to an institutional mentality that welcomes only the elect.

Christ was a gatherer.

All are necessary to make up the full Body of Christ.

Our Catechism teaches that marriage is something that takes place when a man and a woman enter into a sacramental union. That is our belief on marriage. But who would discount that God's kingdom is coming also through the serious commitment of one person to another and the good fruits which come from that love?

Is a case being made by some that we have the authority to limit God's kingdom to those who are in full compliance with all Scriptural teachings? Can we limit God's kingdom to those who are in full compliance to every element of our Catechism?

This cannot be true. It simply cannot be the way. Love is love and true sacrificial love brings about more love. I in no way seek to erase the line between compliance and non-compliance to the teachings of the Catechism. We are objecting to the artificial construct developed by human beings which reinforces a Pharisaic belief system which limits the preparation of the Bride of Christ.

Further, I do not believe, if we look from heaven, we will see such a thing as a line. I believe, from heaven, we will see each person with their crosses trying to manage wounds and weaknesses as they try to fix on their identity in Christ. As beloved children of the Father, we must accept no ugly exclusion of any group of people. We accept, as followers, that we lack full understanding of the condition of any man. Only God can judge.

Now, it is true that some people live in partial compliance and demand that the 'do's and don'ts' be changed. This cannot happen except through the hierarchy of the Church. A demand for change in a spirit of defiance to the prescription is typically not an appropriate spirit or agent. Rather, a steady process of contribution and a dignified dialogue will bring about unity between those who live the prescription and those who disagree with it.

There can also be challenging dialogue between those who are living the prescription but not the Spirit and those who are living the Spirit and not the prescription. For unity to take place, as stated, everyone has to move, if only in their view of others.

To be clear, we should all strive to accept our civic responsibilities as citizens of heaven in *advance* of heaven so that we can help Christ be present in the world.

With regard to the decisions made by our leaders, let it be noted that not everyone agrees with the decisions. This is no cause for war, though, and we should not march into battle against our friends. We certainly wish they would not march into battle against us. And Christ, Himself, would not try to force agreement. He would expect opposition. How did Christ deal with opposition? Well, he held his position of love and He did not depart from the truth. Our leaders defending Church teaching are acting like Christ when they defend the teachings with both firmness and love. And we, as followers, accept and support the leadership even while we understand that not everyone agrees with us and everyone is entitled to be loved and respected as they live out their beliefs.

Also, we, as a community of believers, have an expectation that those believers who are living in partial compliance to the teachings, contribute meaningfully and participate as fully as possible. Christ will be looking for each of us to account for the gifts and talents, the formation and beliefs that He provided for us. We, as Church, must have the same expectation of our brothers and sisters living in partial compliance but perhaps in greater communion of love and indeed, perhaps in greater compliance through a more complete communion of love than many who are in full compliance to the 'do's and don'ts' but live out their non-compliance in the secrecy of pornography/masturbation or cruelty to those closest to them.

The Catechism of the Catholic Church states:

"Mortal sin is a radical possibility of human freedom, as is love itself. It results in the loss of charity and the privation of sanctifying grace, that is, of the state of grace. If it is not redeemed by repentance and God's forgiveness, it causes exclusion from Christ's kingdom and the eternal death of hell, for our freedom has the power to make choices for ever, with no turning back. However, although we can judge that an act is in itself a grave offense, we must entrust judgment of persons to the justice and mercy of God." (CCC 1861)

We must all be willing to examine ourselves, regardless of where we are standing in the safe pasture that is the Church.

Additionally, the doors to the Church, if they are accurately representing Christ, will be open and not only partially open but propped open fully. The upside to this is two-fold. One, light from the Church can stream out, beckoning others. Two, we have transparency.

The downside to such openness is that vandals and brigands often enter and attempt to disrupt the peace inside.

So be it. They will know we are Christians by our love, not, they will know we are Christians by our full and exacting compliance with each sexual teaching of the Church at all times in our lives. If truth be told, nearly none of us could hit the perfect mark there given that the Church's teaching rightfully orders our physical sexual expression to our heavenly citizenship. Any voice making accusations at another should be a very little voice indeed, it would seem to me, and anyone pointing a finger at another's sexual misconduct (excluding criminal behavior) should be one speaking from poverty and trembling in Spirit.

Yes, we are all impoverished given our broken and vulnerable humanity. Christ knew this. And when Christ challenged the Pharisees He did so not because He disliked them. He loved them as He loves all of God's children. But He, as their Savior and for their own sake, had to insist that they be shown the absolute poverty of their perspective.

Jesus Christ desires that each of us accept the same poverty of our perspective as we navigate the call to follow that He sounds in our souls. Only by understanding our poverty, will our preaching of the Gospel message pack the power to draw others back to Christ.

March 22, 2012

It is a paradox that in order to possess the greatest amount of clarity we have to understand the great poverty of our perspective. Every created child of God is called to union with God, even though at times people feel they are forgotten by God. But they are never forgotten by God. "Does a woman forget her baby at her breast or fail to cherish the son of her womb? Yet even if these forget, I will never forget you," (Isaiah 49:8-15).

No, the good God wants all to rejoice with Him and to call others into rejoicing. This includes all who have fallen away, all who live lives which are not in perfect compliance with the prescription of our teachings. Indeed, it is to these especially that the Lord wishes to cry out.

Clearly, we, as Christ bearers, must deliver this message. The message allows for many, many roadways and a highway made from all mountains. The Lord promises to bank up high roads and draw people from all directions. We read that some are coming from further away and that people are coming from different directions and that this is cause for exultation, not division.

My friends, please note that the Scripture references people making a journey. They are not immediately at a destination. They are making their way from one place to another. Are we respectful of that journey? Do we each recognize that we are on a journey ourselves?

I remember a child who moved to a different place. She carried a stuffed animal with her and during the first month of her new life, she would not put the stuffed animal down. She brought it everywhere. The child, having endured the trauma of the move, could not be told that she did not need the stuffed animal or even that she would be happier without carrying the stuffed animal as it was limiting her freedom in ways. What was important was that she believed she could not do without this stuffed animal and when she was told, quite kindly, by a new teacher to put it away, she became upset. The teacher, with wisdom, decided to say nothing about the stuffed animal. When the child began to feel safe and began to recover from the trauma of the move, she eventually left it down for longer and longer periods and eventually it was placed on a shelf as an important part of her history.

Perhaps we should treat those approaching Catholic spirituality in a similar way. They will be bringing things with them. We can greet them by saying, "We do not carry those things here and neither should you". Or we can greet them in exultation, saying things like 'I certainly remember carrying things like that'. We can be mindful of the long journey they may have travelled to reach God. And perhaps, over time, when they see that we have reverence about their baggage and indeed have our own baggage, and understand the pain that causes them to carry it, they will put some things down. But this will be between the person and Christ, mostly. And breaking away from heavy and unnecessary habits, which are sinful, prideful, or just inconsistent with our faith, is usually a process, as we each know.

When we think of the ocean, we can probably get a picture of the Body of Christ. It is in constant motion. For example, study the water. Find the drop of water in the ocean that does not have to move. Which is it? How many of them are there? Search, by looking very closely and try to identify which drop of water can remain perfectly still and still be part of the dynamic, moving, reality that is the sea.

We are the same. If we are to remain authentically part of the Body of Christ, we will be in constant motion. If we are separated from the rest of the Body of Christ, meaning, if we stop self-examining, we will dry up like a drop of water that lands on a rock and is then baked by the sun.

Recognition that every other created child of God is not only in motion but is *called* to be in motion will provide exquisite reverence for how God views His children: all important, all imperfect and all on a journey.

The Compliance Factor

Because truth is objective and our Catechism offers what we believe is the truth about how God wants us to live, we must also accept another truth and that is that we all fail sometimes.

How on earth are we to reconcile this to hope? Clearly, we do so through receiving mercy from God ourselves and then offering that same mercy to others. Our need for God's mercy presupposes that we are not in full compliance to heavenly behavior at all times during our life on earth. This allows us to accept that same reality about others. But there is a distortion coming from some in the Church which leads to the limited thinking that the Church is an exclusive group where only some are suitable for membership.

Let's think of it as the Compliance Factor.

The Compliance Factor is something like a yardstick or an inventory. At any given moment, most of us are not fully compliant in both spirit and letter. Yet we can at times exclude people from the Church because from *our* standpoint they do not appear compliant.

It is up to us to participate in on-going self-evaluation. This is nothing new. This is simply good Christian living. We were taught to examine our conscience at night, not to go to sleep with anxiety because we had failed, but to go to sleep after having offered God the day with the truth of both our weaknesses and our strengths, our failures and successes. We were taught to thank God for the goodness in us and ask God to forgive those moments when we rejected the goodness and chose instead to exercise our freedom by acting against our relationship with God by offering sin instead.

My friends, distortions of this are seen in guilt complexes and outwardly rigid behavior with interior self-hatred. True fruits from this way of life were seen in relaxed people who were kind to themselves and others and who advanced in virtue through practice.

No saint went to heaven with pockets full of condemnation and full reports about the mistakes of those around them. We are all called to be saints. So let us each worry about our own process of advancing in virtue.

As a picture, let us see people as living in some compliance. I believe that is what God sees, truly. I believe that until the very moment a sinner rejects God and all of us in God's family and insists on going to hell, that God has hope for repentance and that God is open to seeing just where each person is getting it right.

Consider a prisoner. He is convicted of murder. (For the record, people can be wrongly convicted. Christ was.) That sinner repents and pursues holiness in prison. When he dies, does God view him as only partially compliant? Or does God welcome him as someone who is 'ready to go' heaven-wise because of the long and exacting work that prisoner pursued after his crime.

Only God knows.

Think of a man living in a same-sex relationship. He is a doctor who serves in the military. He ministers to soldiers on his side of the conflict, soldiers on the other side of the conflict and any civilians who wander through his care by chance. He loves God's children and does not discriminate between them. He dies. Does God focus only on the acting out of the sexual attraction? Is it possible that the God of mercy and love would ignore the pattern of mercy and love that this man flowed through his healing craft? I cannot imagine this and none of my experience of God would point to this.

A couple is living in an irregular union. They are committed, monogamous, and care with precision and love to the duties between them, meaning children, careers etc. For whatever reasons, their union is not regularized according to our Church teaching. Their children, however, are catechized and know and understand the situation of their parents. One partner dies. Does God then reject the person because their union was not regularized?

My friends, this is frighteningly limited thinking. Unless that person rejects God and the family of God, that person will be spending eternity with us. And there can be many reasons why unions are not regularized.

Offering a person his or her non-compliance in the Church does not always provide that person with an experience of God's mercy. People can be made to feel that if they lack the prescription (of the law), then they will be denied the medicine (mercy).

If we think of ministry as spiritual medicine, then perhaps we can understand we are offering Christ as the doctor of the soul. Different patients will require different medicine. We would not offer someone who spoke only English a teaching written in Chinese. The person would not understand the language and would go away frustrated, possibly feeling he was hopelessly inadequate to the task.

Many people returning to the Church do not know the

Catechism or what it teaches. What would the merciful Christ want from those who represent Him? The greatest possible offering of mercy, one would think.

I remember a little boy going into the hospital for dehydration. He was terribly feverish and his mouth was painfully dry. The doctor inserted the intravenous fluids and then gave the little boy a Popsicle. He told the mother, "He will probably throw it up but we want to let him taste the hydration we're giving him. That way, he will feel happy and relaxed."

The doctor was concerned about the patient's experience of getting well. He desired to give the little boy immediate comfort, even though he knew it was not the full answer or indeed any answer at all, given his condition. The intravenous line was the answer ultimately, and the doctor was providing that, but the Popsicle consoled the boy, gave him hope, and helped him to taste what the care would ultimately provide, more complete hydration.

We, too, must be gravely concerned about the immediate experience of those seeking reconciliation with the Church. Presenting with the half empty scenario, that is, "Here is where you are not compliant and therefore not suitable for entry" is contrary to the goal which will always be reconciliation of some description with the Body of Christ. But the most important part is that the person *feels* the benefit of the reconciliation immediately, just like the boy tasted the coldness and soothing liquid of the Popsicle. The little boy ultimately got well and he, via the Popsicle, had an immediate understanding that the hospital was a good place for him.

I believe there must be offered a pathway to compliance, a clearly marked process offering those returning a road on which to journey and build spiritual muscle. We must do our best to communicate to each person that they are loved, important, necessary, and yes, also accountable.

For example, it is true that many people depart from compliance by degrees of separation. So…a marriage fails. Both are wounded. One begins a relationship with another person. The new couple move in together and begin living life as a family with children from one or both. They are now looking like a family and indeed living family life but without the Sacramental graces of matrimony.

This is not ideal but it is happening frequently.

At that time, we have a perilous moment. Will they abandon all practice? Will they stop catechizing their children? Offering their children the Sacraments as the children move through development? It depends. Do they feel welcome to live out their spirituality in the Church in these less than ideal circumstances?

Arguably, they are making a choice to live away from compliance to the teachings of the Church and the consequence is…what is the consequence? This is very important. We have so many wounds and injuries in this current time. These wounds are psychological, mental, emotional and spiritual. Some people are wounded in all of those areas. Often, they are doing the best they can with the circumstances they have encountered in their lives. We must accept that where they may be non-compliant in some ways they may be excelling in others.

The tricky part about all of this is that nothing needs to change but our thinking. Christ is and always has been merciful. The Church teaching allows for process. But we must repackage the mercy the Church offers so that it can be understandable to those in need of it. They must see that mercy is there for them, that they are worthy of it and indeed that it was given for their circumstances.

A woman travelling in a foreign country once bought a can of margarine because it had a picture of an apple pie on the cover. Imagine her disappointment. In the same way, we must be honest about Church teaching and the condition in which many find themselves so there is no confusion about what God wants for us and what God needs to keep us as safe as possible. But we must also help people to understand that there is a path into sainthood with their name on it. And if that path is within our Church, we must direct them to it. It may be that their journey to complete unity with the Sacraments will be delayed by an irregular union but that is no reason why their spirituality should not advance with all speed.

We cannot stamp people or entire families with stamps that say 'Non-Compliant' and give up.

This simply cannot be the way. Perhaps each reader will ponder this subject and consider how to best offer something better.

Locution from Diocesan Priest from Heaven

Priest from Heaven

The words of a priest who served in a diocese during his life.

April 3, 2012
In my life, I was ordained to the priesthood. It was the course I chose because of the prompting I heard in my spirit. In my life time, I served well, though often I limited God by my unwillingness to go more deeply into my prayer life. The result of this was that I did not advance as much as I might have and as much as God wanted me to advance. Yet, the grace God sent through me amazes me when I study it from heaven.

On entering eternity, I was startled. I found myself surrounded by truth and this truth included the truth about my prayer life and the consequence of my prayer life on my soul's development. I could have gone further into the love of Jesus Christ while I was on earth. It was there for me. My lack of awareness was not the problem in that God limits our awareness so that we can gain merit through our service. Additionally, I can see that being separated from God would be even more difficult if we had greater awareness. Those who possess greater awareness of God suffer very much from the separation while they remain on earth.

Still, I had every means available to me through a committed prayer life and I treated it casually at times, and, I am sorry to say, with contempt at some moments. This is true and I am not afraid to admit it because I do not want other priests to suffer as I suffered when I found myself in eternity and faced the fact that I could have done better. Despite the limitations, that I took full responsibility for, God cared for His children through me during my ministry on earth. God's love is so exquisite that He works on, even though at times priests actually ridicule the ministry He has entrusted to them. Only a determined love would continue to flow grace through a man who harbored ridicule for the Father in his soul.

I suffered all of this upon my arrival into eternity. But now I am being rewarded for my perseverance despite my trials and faults. Brothers, please, for the sake of the Father and His children, and

*for the sake of your own soul, be painstaking about your prayer life
and ask the Spirit to come to you throughout each day. Rely on the
Spirit and follow Him with zeal because I tell you, the Spirit is
with you and in you and desires that you be like small children
receiving love from the God of the Eucharist so that you can be
transformed into Jesus Himself who walked the earth distributing
love. If you do not feel a Father's tender pity when you look out at
the souls entrusted to you, then you must go back to your prayer
life and ask for it.*

*Suffer the periods of trial quietly, but do not spread anything
but conviction to the men serving alongside you. Let them scoff at
your conviction if they must but inside they will admire it and try
to find it for themselves when they see it in you. My brothers, you
will thank me for these words if you heed them. If you do not heed
them, you will suffer as I suffered. I want to spare you if I can.
God's mercy is available to you in these few words and God's mercy
is available to you in the graces I am securing for you as you read
them.*

*Because I am in eternity now, having suffered for the smallest
time in Purgatory, I can gain for you a richness of grace through
your prayers to me. I want to do this for you because I want you to
have all that is available to you in your prayer life. I am happy as
I contemplate what God will give you if you ask Him for help. I
have no regrets any longer because I am using all that was good
about my life to gain graces for those of you who remain. If you
could see what is waiting for you in heaven, as priests, you would
begin living your heaven while you served on earth, as Father to
God's children. You would be joyful each day, despite the trials.*

*Brothers, do not pay much attention to external difficulties. The
world does not understand us. Be more alert to the interior
difficulties and work on those. Being ridiculed by the world is a gift
to us. It can only help us if our prayer life is right. Words will not
help here, I am afraid, but grace is available and I am asking for it
for you.*

*Be happy as you work. God is exactly what He needs to be even
if you are not and if you do as I say and hasten into the silence of
prayer, you will grow quickly. Many of you are better than I was*

on earth. *This makes me happy. I admire you and I am grateful that you are using the tools God has given you.*

But some of you need these words and I am watching closely to help you. Be filled with confidence. God is strong. One man who is determined in the Spirit can affect so much and can turn a diocese into a heavenly kingdom of its own. I can see this from heaven.

Do your part, brothers. We are working together.

Our Lady, Queen of the Church

Mary, our Mother, has many titles. One of them is Mother of the Church. In this beautiful reference we see that maternity and protection come from Our Lady as she ministers to the Body of Christ serving on earth.

In this time, the Church is challenged to move into a dynamic period of renewal. Renewal will require each Catholic to attach himself to the ever present power of the Holy Spirit and allow God to draw from him graces of love and evangelization. Only an active and co-responsible laity can insure swift advance in this regard. This change is necessary if the Church is to respond positively and decisively to the confusion experienced by God's children in the face of both subtle and direct challenges to our Way. While, as Catholics, we seek to obtain and to retain the freedom to practice our faith, we must also consider that we believe Christianity has the obligation in the world to represent God's highest hopes for the dignity of humanity.

This is a serious obligation.

For this reason and this purpose, it would seem that the Lord desires that His most holy mother became known as Our Lady, Queen of the Church. Venerated in this way, she will intercede with specific graces for the protection and growth of the Church on earth. The Church will benefit through Mary's dignity as Queen of the Church, but also through her influence and authority as Queen of the Church. Honoring the feminine authority of Mary as Queen will provide for all Catholics a spotless call, drawing them further into service in the Church, not as passive participants but as meaningful and active contributors who, like Mary, can help protect the course of all of humanity by humble service to the King's wishes through fidelity to the Magisterium.

Our Lady, Queen of Apostles, Queen of Saints, Queen of Angels, Queen of Peace and Queen of Heaven and Earth is already, by virtue of being the mother of the King, a Queen. Chosen by the Creator to remain immaculate, she chose never to be separated from the will of the Trinity and it is for this reason that she should be venerated as Queen of the Church. Who, like Mary, can draw God's children back into purity as a reciprocal gift of love to the Father? Who, like Mary, can properly model the necessary strength and humility of women as they live out their commitments to Jesus Christ our King?

Mary, mother of the King, can be an approachable first stop for those seeking reconciliation with the Sacramental life of the Church and her intercession as Queen of the Church during this period will restore many to the Sacraments.

There are those who express a feminine wound in the Church. Certainly, the times prompt equality and dignity between men and women. In heaven there is most assuredly this equality and dignity which we desire on earth but imperfectly strive to achieve. By offering the truth about Mary's role in the Church, that is, acknowledging her Queenship therein, we will help to heal people from a wound and direct them to a model. We will more brightly illuminate an existing path.

By venerating Mary as Queen of the Church, we will allow God to teach us more about the complementarity of the genders.

It is hoped that the woman entering service to the Church will view herself, like Mary, as essential to the life and growth of the Church. The woman entering service to the Church will recognize the beauty of complementarity as essential, and not incidental, to the spread of the Gospel Message.

It is hoped that the man entering service to the Church will view himself as a bold proclaimer of Jesus Christ in the world as well as in the Church, and as someone who acts with Jesus to protect and defend Mary, the Queen of the Church. The man entering service to the Church will recognize and defend the essential role of women, not only in the Church but also in the world and, so preciously, in the family.

Clearly, God reveals Himself and His plan for the Church into the Church over time. The preparation of the Bride of Christ advances and into each time God sends the remedies and protection for all challenges to the proper development of the Church. We, as Catholics, must be alert to the Spirit who seeks to both defend and advance in that we simultaneously protect what is truth and advance further into that truth. In other words, further development in the present of that which we have received in the past is no threat, and indeed, only verifies the true nature of our beliefs.

Therefore, with confidence in God's presence in this historical period of time, we respond to what we believe is His desire that Our Lady, Queen of Apostles, Queen of Saints, Queen of Angels, Queen of Peace and Queen of Heaven and Earth also be venerated as Our Lady, Queen of the Church.

We have the great joy and privilege of welcoming the image of Our Lady Queen of the Church. A copy of the image can be found on the inside back cover of this book. I want to describe for you some of the components of the image and the related symbolism. This description is not in order of priority.

The icon, first of all, introduces Our Lady as Queen of the Church. Why do we believe the Lord is calling for the spread of both the title and the image?

The times prompt equality and dignity between men and women. In heaven, there is most assuredly this equality and dignity which we desire on earth but have yet to achieve. By offering the truth about Mary's role in the Church, we will help, hopefully, to heal some people from a wound and direct us all to a model.

We know that the Church is developing over time. And we know that Our Lady is very important to us now because we so urgently need renewal in the Church.

The images of Jesus Christ the Returning King and Our Lady Queen of the Church may be hung side by side to represent the complementarity of the genders. Our Catechism teaches that in creating man, male and female, God gives men and women an equal personal dignity. He wants this in the Church and out of the Church.

You will see that Our Lady's right hand is in a similar teaching and instructing position as the Lord's right hand in the image of Jesus Christ the Returning King. Both the feminine and the masculine teach the truth, but often in different ways. We need both.

Her left hand supports the Church and the Church is seen as a humble, simple building. The doors are open, the windows also. There is transparency, and, we pray, humility. When I say Church, please do not think of only clergy. WE are ALL the Church. We need to be transparent about our beliefs and also our imperfection and our journey. The whole Church, in order to represent Jesus Christ accurately, needs more humility. All of us. Our Lady will help us with this and prompt us gently toward very humble service to the people around us.

The many bells on the roof represent the Church in every country. I saw, in a vision, on top of the Church, a bell for every country. Each was meant to ring out a distinct harmonious note. I saw that there were weeds coming up through the inside of the Church and they were interfering with the movement and function of the bells in various countries. In other countries the bell was ringing functionally and sounding the right note, meaning, the Church in that country was accurately representing heaven. In other countries, the Church was being misrepresented and therefore people could not see the beauty of our faith. Overall, the bells were not sounding together and creating the type of harmony that the Lord wants. I saw that it was Our Lady's role to bring the bells into harmony, meaning, to restore and renew the Church in each country and to bring about consistency.

Now, consistency does not mean conformity. You can see in the lower left foreground that there are three sets of bells. These represent the Church in different countries and the colors are notably different. The subtle difference in the colors indicates the unique personality of the Church in each country. This is good. The Church in each country must transform into its highest representation of Church. We must contemplate ourselves as Catholics and also nationally so that we can express our unique selves in the international Church. The Irish Church will look a little different than the African Church and the Chinese Church will hold its beautiful Chinese expression and still function in the same way as the American Church only singing out a little differently. We have a great deal, always, to learn from each other.

We see Our Lady indicating the bells on the top of the Church. It is her project to renew the Church in each country and she must be known in each country individually as the Queen of that country.

Our Lord holds the scepter of Kingship in the image of Jesus

Christ the Returning King. Our Lady, through her humanity, offers us the truth that the Church on earth is incarnational and meant to be presented and represented daily through our human representation modeled after her spotless call. The fact that we imperfectly represent God's perfection should not deter us from a spirited preaching of the Gospel message.

Our Lady, the Queen of the Church is issuing an invitation to all Catholics to return to the Sacramental life of the Church.

The diocesan structure of the Church is represented by the intricate and rich hem of her garment which encircles her mantle, just as the Church encircles the earth. The church is held in the hand of Mary, near her heart and offered to the world from the hand of a woman so that we can see that women are essential to the life and growth of the Church and impact profoundly how the Church is both presented to the world and viewed by the world. The Queen of the Church is inviting all women to emulate her strength and humility and she is asking men to protect and promote the role of women, in the Church, yes, and also in the world and, of infinite importance, in the family. We must advance together in unity or we will not advance.

Now, the diocesan structure of the Church is very important in this time. For renewal to take place quickly, it will have to happen more or less simultaneously in every diocese around the world. This is why lay apostles are urged to pray for their bishop and be part of their diocese in some way. Our children must know which diocese they come from and understand that they are part of something from heaven, here on earth.

Our Lady's beautiful hands represent her humanity and the teaching of the Assumption that she was brought into heaven both body and soul. She sits on a silver throne, different to the Lord's. This emphasizes that she is separate from the Trinity, a created human being, simultaneously subordinate to God and elevated by God. While God created her immaculately for her role as the first tabernacle, Mary contributed an ongoing yes answer and made a choice to remain immaculate. In doing so, she enclosed herself in the divine will which is represented in the closure of the clasp of her belt with the silver fleur de lei, symbolizing the Trinity. Her whole humanity and life were enclosed in service to the Church on earth.

Indeed, Mary is a living symbol of obedience and models for us the same call of obedience to the teachings and leadership of the Magisterium of the Church. She is directing us all to this obedience in a special way in this time.

On her silver crown there is a large blue stone, the most prominent. This represents her maternity, both human and through her human maternity to Jesus, divine. She was a human mother who nourished a little baby and she is a spiritual mother who nourishes all of Gods' children. Above the blue stone is the smaller red stone which represents her participation in the Passion of Jesus. This stone honors her role in the redemption of humanity and is an example to each of us that our sufferings are both meaningful and important. We suffer with Jesus, as Mary did, for the Church on earth. As Janusz, the artist said, "one year of suffering went into the creation of this image."

On each side of the blue stone we see two emerald green stones which represent the four vocations in the Church, namely married, single, religious and clergy. The stones are of equal size and value to the Queen because each vocation is necessary for her to complete her task of the renewal of the whole Church on earth. The stones in Our Lady's crown signify how she contributed to the Church in her life. The green stones signify how we contribute to the Church on our life.

Co-responsibility must be accepted by every person in each vocation because each vocation must play a unique part in the advancement of the Church into its final preparation as the Bride of Christ.

Below right is an image of the Holy Father kneeling before Mary as Queen of the Church. On the back of his vestment are the keys to the kingdom representing the ongoing papal role and asking that each pope seek guidance and protection from the Queen.

We see the wheat and grapes in the border, representing the Eucharist.

Lastly, we have the beautiful flowers at her feet, representing what Saint Pope John Paul II called the new springtime.

In the end, Our Lady, Queen of the Church, will bring about harmony, consistency and renewal in the Church throughout the world.

Thoughtful Men and Women of God

"With what sweetness I have returned my will to Him! Yes, I want Him to take charge of my faculties in such a way that my actions will no longer be human...but divine, inspired and directed by the Spirit of love." St. Therese of Liseux

Thoughtful Men and Women of God

It is clear that we, in contemporary society, suffer from a malady which can obstruct our ability to focus on God. This malady can also go so far as to diminish our ability to adequately calm ourselves. We can think of this as mind pollution. This occurs when our minds become filled with information and material which is not of God. These negative things can include impure images, impure entertainment or even impure conversations. Impure conversations are those which are not connected to a good agenda.

If our minds are full of the things of this world, created by man, then our minds are like cluttered workshops with environmental hazards left everywhere. In a messy and cluttered workshop filled with contaminants, a person will not work as well as if he is in a clean and ventilated workshop filled with good natural light and tools which best serve His craft. Also, if a person feels confident and free in his workshop, he will be more creative and efficient.

My friends, the condition of the workshop that is our minds directly impacts our ability to experience Jesus in our souls. As such, we must keep our minds clean and well-ventilated by the Holy Spirit. If we are to serve Christ effectively, if we are to be true servants to the King who seeks to return, then we must enable our minds to contemplate God in our soul and allow Him dominion there. In this way, He will be able to teach us how to best allow Him to flow through us into the world. Jesus is the master craftsman of love, after all, and we must spend time with Him so He can teach us. This teaching is necessarily one-on-one. Are we showing up for our personal tutorials?

The lessons, I believe, for this time must be learned in contemplative prayer. Given our collective backdrop of information overload, contemplative prayer must be the answer and the mandate. It is the healing agent and the touchstone.

Because our actions, taken directly from our thoughts and not contemplated against God's directions for us personally on each day, will be random. Even if we make objectively good decisions, these decisions may not be what God needs to come through us into His kingdom on this day. For example, attending a prayer group is a good thing, but not if God needs us sitting with a dying or hurting family member or neighbor.

As apostles, we want the best for our King. We want to give Him the greatest fidelity. In order to ensure that, we must allow Him to use our minds with the greatest effectiveness to transform our souls and direct us personally.

Therefore, and with reverence for our personal relationship with Christ, we embark on a journey of freedom. We can be imprisoned physically, mentally, emotionally or spiritually and yet we can be free if we allow Jesus to reign as King in our thoughts and in our souls. We know that many saints were led from prison cells to their deaths rejoicing in God's Kingship and in their own conviction that, while condemned on earth, they were going to a place where they were free. How did they do this? Why would they claim triumph when they were utterly without hope of liberation?

They claimed freedom in advance, despite dire earthly circumstances, because they, through contemplation of Christ, were free. We can each have this same freedom. It is ours to claim. But we must decide to do so.

How does one become free?

I believe it is one's perception, to a large part, which determines one's condition. What we believe about ourselves, we become. What is the truth about each one of us? We were created to do good things. And it is true that we, though imperfect, desire good to a greater or lesser degree. Even the desire to have the desire to do good things is evidence of our goodness and enough for us to start the journey. If we can accept that we are likely to make mistakes and that we have indeed made mistakes in the past, but despite our mistakes we would like to advance further into virtue, then we are on the right track to becoming important servants to the King in the world.

Now, in the same way that we will never become a saint by studying sin, we will never become free by studying slavery. We must be sure that in our souls we soar into the heavens rather than remain with our eyes fixed on the gravity which holds our feet to the earth. We *are* free if we direct our thoughts into freedom. The decision, all by itself, draws our eyes into heaven.

Christ needs this, my friends, because we, the sheep, can be easily scattered, through our own frailty and through the frailty of others. But if we are each independently connected to the one true Shepherd, we cannot be scattered and we will recognize each other and also recognize those who are not connected to the Shepherd. This helps us to distinguish between those with whom we should serve and those with whom we should not serve.

Learning is all about repetition. This is neurological fact. For that reason, we must practice being saints. We must practice being contemplatives in the world or out of the world, wherever we find ourselves. Only through contemplating our circumstances with Jesus each day, in the freedom of our souls, will we prepare for the next world and help to bring about the changes we are meant to bring about in this world. If we free our minds, our bodies will calm, the urges which distract us will quiet nicely and we will rest peacefully in our souls.

A thoughtful man or woman of God spends a great deal of time in the silence of his soul, even in a crowded room. Silence is not just about the absence of sound or hearing, it is about the decision to focus on something different. When we practice silence as a decision, with a purpose of encountering God, we exercise the supernatural sense. Thus, we can live silence in any condition, even when we have difficulty getting large periods of physical silence. The supernatural sense is one we share but one that has been largely ignored in this time, much like an unworked or atrophied muscle. A deluge of information bombards our physical senses daily and our minds simply cannot empty it all fast enough to rest in the supernatural sense that is our intuitive knowledge and connection to God. My goodness. Such a state of affairs! The wise man busies himself immediately once he identifies the task.

Let us embark with no further delay.

Formula for Contemplative Prayer

To begin, we set aside ten minutes per day for this new, special contemplative prayer. People seeking God find Him everywhere but this ten minutes is in addition to all other prayer practices. It is a new tuition, an extra class, an adjunct study.

Sit quietly for a minute or so. Close your eyes. Give your body a chance to drop into the action of stopping. All activity ceases. All electronic devices are silenced. You are a spiritual being with a temporary human body, created to do good things and God is hoping you will look His way for direction. You are doing exactly that right now. All is well.

While breathing, slowly, and deeply, (make sure your stomach is moving) count backwards from ten. There is no prize for getting to one fast. Go slowly. You are succeeding simply by your decision for contemplative prayer. Allow calm understanding to be yours. You are a child of God seeking God and everything is exactly as it should be in this moment. Lovely.

When you get to one, say to yourself, "Body, relax. It is time to pray. Mind, be still. Jesus is coming." Say this three times in a friendly, loving way. You would not speak to a child harshly. We are all children. We must speak to our minds and bodies lovingly.

Next, direct all of your attention to your soul. It is not just your brain and it is not just your mind, although these things influence and impact your soul. Your soul is the part of you that can never be caged. It is the space where you and God are together and can work together to protect your relationship with Him and to protect His plan for your life. You can picture your soul as a large room, a heavenly workshop. All of your experiences are represented there and all of your actions. All of the information you are taking in has a space in your soul. Initially, if your mind is cluttered and you are new to this experience, you can feel somewhat disoriented in this type of prayer exercise. It can take a little time. But you are committed to taking charge of your mind and using it to rest with God in your soul. God is committed to helping you succeed. Also, we are acting on God's prompting, so we are guaranteed to succeed if we first, begin and then, persevere.

Now, picture a person standing with their nose pressed to a

mountain. They remain in this position and it is their first experience of the mountain.

When we begin contemplative prayer, this can be us. This is fine. Even in this position, we are learning.

Pretend the mountain is God. His presence is enormous. He is always with you and He most certainly wants to help you to direct your mind to Him so you can work with Him. He wants to be King of your mind and He created you to be loved and supported by Him.

Your eyes are closed. Your body is still.

Here come the distractions! Unruly thoughts, memories and observations, random and disconnected, can pelt themselves at your awareness when you try to calm down, but now you are directing your mind to the clear space of your soul that is always available to the created one and the Creator. When the thoughts come, simply picture yourself picking them up and putting them on a shelf, to look at later if you decide you need to do so. For now, stay in the spacious room reserved for you and Jesus.

The room is so big and relaxed. It is such a relief to be there. Picture a little child set down gently in an empty ballroom. He looks so small and unsure at first.

You are similar here. You are small and the space of your soul is large, limitless. But rather than this being a frightening thing, this is a marvelous thing. The possibilities are literally endless in this room. It is safe…so, so safe. You were always meant to be here with God.

Maybe you spent a lot of time with a racing mind in the past. Maybe there was a fast beat that took hold of your life and every time you tried to think, this fast beat took you, quickening your heart instead of quieting it. But in this place of your soul, spacious and safe, comfortable and warm, the beat is slow and rhythmic. The beat is reassuring and abundantly calming. It neither starts nor finishes. It is. And you are part of it and it is part of you. You belong in this nourishing heartbeat of Jesus. The God heartbeat is one which we recognize and crave. If we have lost it, we are like wandering sheep. When we find it again, we feel gratitude. It is only in this beat that we truly relax on earth. We can think of this as the heartbeat of the Sacred Heart which pumps steadily in the Place of the Divine Will. (For more on this see *Serving in Clarity*).

Now, when you are in your soul, with Jesus, for this special work, you expend little effort. Rather, you are led. Jesus Christ, Himself, will direct your prayer experience. You will know it is working if you notice that Jesus is leading you to decisions and conclusions which resonate in the Place of the Divine Will. Because, my friends, your soul is the Place of the Divine Will if you follow Christ. And that is why we must together make a commitment to 'do the hard work in our heads', as Immaculee Ilibagiza said when confronted with the fact that her family's killers were also her brothers and sisters in Christ and thus had to be forgiven and loved. Our hard work in our heads will be different each day, even though some projects will take longer than others. We fear nothing. We are not directors in this room. Christ directs and He, if allowed, will bring us all to healing and sanctity.

On some days we will run to this place, with a problem, a worry, or a feeling of remorse. There with Jesus we will untie the knots, or, as one, holy priest said, "In life we have mixed motives. Prayer is where we go to un-mix our motives."

Thoughtful men and women of God are balanced, according to their time, culture and vocation. They neither become upset by their own sinfulness nor the sinfulness of others. A thoughtful man or woman of God knows that his value is inestimable and much greater than the sum of all of his sinfulness. If the value of what one contributes or the value of even the potential of what one might contribute in the future is inestimable, then why would one become stuck on one's sinfulness?

In the past, when some people focused on sinfulness, they became obsessed with sin. This did not draw others to Christ. It repelled people from Christ. This negative spirituality can take root for many reasons, all of them understandable but none of them worth living a life of perceived spiritual failure.

Negative spirituality goes something like this, 'You were bad in the past, you are blemished today and you are capable of even worse sin in the future. Why try? God is unreasonable and the bar is too high.'

If a person thought like this, he or she could not bear the extent of the burden imposed on self. This thinking can spiral down and a person can become less and less able or even willing to receive mercy. When a person becomes unwilling to receive mercy, that person decides not to desire mercy. Pride comes in and the person can become disparaging of mercy. "I don't need mercy", we might hear.

Now, truthfully, without the ability to receive mercy, a person is not inclined to grant mercy to others. And in an effort to relieve oneself of the weight of this self-condemnation and self-loathing, one, perhaps without awareness, might seek relief by asking others to carry some of the weight. How? By imposing their self-belief on others. What does this look like? Are we describing a Pharisee?

Perhaps the inner dialogue would go something like this: 'In the past I have failed objectively in my spirit. I do not want to admit to my wounds. It is too painful and humbling. The result was sin. Today, I am concealing the scope of my spiritual struggle and outwardly following the prescription of the law. ("You have nothing on me.") I, in my tireless searching, have found an area where you are imperfect. This affords me with the greatest relief and so I will focus my attention on your 'flaw' to take my attention off the fact that I am also imperfect. The more insecure I am, the more I will trumpet your imperfection, real or imagined by me. This takes the attention off me nicely and holds my terror of being shamed, either by self or others, in abeyance.'

Psychologists call this projection. We can all be inclined to do this at times, which is why we need to be extremely self-aware.

The next sentence must be read carefully.

The greater the disagreement between how we act and what we secretly believe about ourselves, the greater the likelihood that we will project our negative self-beliefs on to someone else.

In the most extreme form, we can have a superiority addict, or, as Christ states in Scripture, someone who "strains out gnats and swallows camels", meaning, possibly, a closet bad actor. This is someone who likes to appear righteous but who secretly behaves with cruelty and judgment toward someone else or, sadly, toward many others.

Jesus was very directly opposed to this duplicitous and

inauthentic way of living. Specifically the Lord said, "'Alas for you, scribes and Pharisees, you hypocrites! You who pay your tithe of mint and dill and cumin and have neglected the weightier matters of the Law-justice, mercy, good faith! These you should have practiced, without neglecting the others. You blind guides! Straining out gnats and swallowing camels! (Matthew 23: 23-25)

My friends, we must avoid self-examination without mercy and we must discipline ourselves to practice contemplative prayer. Contemplative prayer is the answer for the current calamities of mind pollution, self-loathing and the problem of the pagan beat. Why do I use that term?

Generally, Christians like to think of themselves as spiritually motivated. And as Christians, we truly want to be spiritually motivated. Some of us may remember a time when those who did not know about Jesus would have been identified, perhaps judgmentally or perhaps matter-of-factly, by Christians, as Pagans, or, to use the Merriam-Webster definition, "1: Heathen; 2: one who has little or no religion and who delights in sensual pleasures and material goods".

Fellow apostles, it is clear to me that many of us who are trying to follow our faith could easily now be identified as pagans. Why? How have we lapsed into practicing our faith on the surface, even while we continue to seek material goods along with endless entertainment and distraction? How have we departed from right thinking to the degree that we often eat almost exclusively for pleasure and fail to keep our bodies healthy? In what way do we justify watching pornography, either with pornography dedicated web sites or films or even on ordinary television, and fail to see the horrendous chasm between what we claim to be and those practices which we actually adhere to?

This might be something we could identify as the Pagan Beat. We are resonating at a vibration of this world instead of the next world, which I think of as the 'real world', eternity. Some focused religions make it their practice each day to prepare for the next life in heaven. Do we? We should. One thing we are guaranteed in life is death. Given this certainty, would we not want to contribute positively as much as possible to life on this planet for all of our brothers and sisters alive and yet to come? And about brothers and sisters, would we want them treated like the piteous people are treated in pornographic movies? If not, then how can we possibly justify watching others being sacrificed to someone's greed and then someone else's lust?

It seems to me that pornography is as diabolical as human sacrifice. The question must be asked in this time: Who are the pagans? And why would we consider ourselves more advanced than a non-follower if we are behaving secretly or openly in this manner?

It is known in our time that neuroplasticity is our brain's ability to change. We, humanity, can direct the changes in our brain or in the brains of those around us. We know this and remember it as we consider the aggressive rehabilitation we begin on those who have suffered strokes or traumatic brain injuries. We know that our children's brains are physically shaped through love and also through trauma. This is the reality of neuroplasticity.

Pornography is a neuroplastic catastrophe and a neuroplastic train wreck. Pay heed. Our brain is affected through pornography in the same place where heroin affects the brain of heroin users. If we are addicted to pornography, meaning, to be clear, a regular user, then we are similar to a heroin addict. We must not normalize this activity, nor accept that it is natural or helpful to anyone. Rather, a periodic engagement must be viewed as a sin and a regular engagement must be viewed as a sin, an addiction and also a significant psychological issue which could require external support as one begins the necessary process of disengaging from it.

Now, as with any sin, we seek out the human wound which prompted the action. Therefore in the case of an ongoing pornography habit, we will find a deep wound which is demanding attention. So be it. This healing work is our life's most important work.

When we normalize an activity like this, we are not fooling Jesus or anyone in the next world, all of whom are aware of us on our journey. And it seems that modern man has been degraded to a degree which now requires an enormous effort of evangelization which includes human development.

Clearly, we need a Rescue Mission. Mercifully, Jesus has

orchestrated one.

We have looked briefly at the problem of the 'Pagan beat'. We have done this, not to discourage us, but so that we can spring board from the problem, limited, into the unlimited arena of the solution, contemplative prayer.

In contemplative prayer we will be drawn ever so steadily into the Trinitarian existence. The Trinitarian existence is the highest hope that the Father, Son and Holy Spirit holds for each one of us, even during our time on earth in exile. The Trinity seeks to educate, nourish and sustain us, each according to their divine role and overall nature of love. The reality that the Father, the Son and the Holy Spirit seek to remain with us in every moment of our time on earth should fill us with confidence. We are drawn ever so steadily into the relationship that exists between these three Persons.

Through proximity to Jesus Christ, we will be transformed into holy men or women of God. If we are following the prescription of the law, it is good. But we need to absorb large amounts of the Spirit of the Law, the Holy Spirit, through our Vertical Relationship with Christ and thus we will fulfil the hopes of the Father who contemplated us into existence.

Our minds are the battle ground in this particular campaign. Take up the sword, apostles!

If a battle raged in front of us, and we were holding a sword, and someone very vulnerable, someone we loved, was getting brutally assaulted, we would most likely step in, wield our sword and try to assist the victim.

My friends, we are that victim. We are assaulted each day in ways that disturb our peace, diminish our dignity and weaken our resolve to help God. This is serious and we are in the battle of our lives, for our lives and for the lives of others. There are many levels in between but let us take two obvious points of reference.

One is music. Perhaps the reader remembers a time when a certain song or melody got 'stuck' in one's head and played over and over. Try though we might, we could not stop our mind from replaying a song, even if we hated the song, or perhaps especially if we hated the song. This could be annoying at the least. At the most, it could consume us and cause us terrible mental suffering.

Another experience of our mind could be a traumatic event.

When trauma occurs, our mind has the job of making sense of it. Sometimes, the trauma can play, over and over. In the worst circumstances, when we are too young to recognize what was done to us, understand its impact on us or accept that we were not cogently responsible, we can begin to live from the wound, meaning, we have a distorted understanding and belief about ourselves and others.

This affects everything.

These are two examples of what can happen in our minds. One is rather small, the song replaying, but through it we can see that the mind likes repetition, can get stuck, and, without training, can replay endlessly. Also, we can see that there are levels of this experience ranging from mild annoyance all the way to an addiction to something like pornography.

The other, the experience of a trauma, is larger and more serious and through it we can see that without understanding our pain and acknowledging our need for healing, we can live lives where we fail to reverence our self or recognize our dignity in God. We can then risk distorting the truth about others, also.

This is terribly serious, indeed, but God sends healing through many avenues. He is always trying to comfort us and give us the truth and the true picture of ourselves and others.

The base truth is that we are generally good people created to do good things. The base truth is that each man or woman on earth is related to us because God created us all. We are all part of one family. In each person, God has placed potential for sanctity. We are meant to help others develop their potential. That is the long and short of it. At the very least, we help others by not hurting them, directly or indirectly. The spirit of destruction is not from God.

So how then must we proceed, given the distractibility of our minds, the reality of our wounds and the mandate we have been given to do good things?

One, we discipline our minds by keeping out the 'songs' we should not be playing and by this we reference all entertainment that would offend God. Replace these things with beautiful music, art and entertainment. Listening to holy chanting or even chanting or singing ourselves can replace some of the more damaging repetitions from which we suffer.

Two, we acknowledge our wounds and take responsibility for working with God until we have received from God the grace to forgive others for the hurts they have inflicted on us and until we have been able to accept healing. If we do this, we will minimize the risk of being a negative, hurtful influence to others.

Three, we get on with our purpose in life, transforming in Christ and serving God on earth by loving and assisting others.

We will understand how God needs us to do that each day through contemplative prayer.

As stated previously, it is possible that we can be tempted to self-hatred because of a misunderstanding about negative experiences we have had and our reactions to those experiences. This can lead to over-scrupulosity. We should be examining our consciences, yes, regularly and well. And we should be doing so according to the formula which, to condense, includes a connection of each sin to the humanity which prompted it.

Formula for Self-Examination

For example, I was afraid and then I did this _____. I was addicted and then I did this _____. I felt rejected and then I did this _____. I was hungry and then I did this ____. I was assaulted and then I did this ____. I was un-parented, rudderless, confused and then I did this ____. I did not take responsibility for my strong emotions and then I did this _____. I stopped self-examining and then I began to behave this way _____.

To be clear, this is not to make excuses for ourselves. This formula helps us to gain self –awareness.

Each person can adapt this but the practice is one which ensures an experience of mercy. One can hardly condemn oneself when one sees that our human weaknesses and our inclinations toward sin are understandable given our wounds. And if one practices understanding others in this way, also, one will be compassionate to others.

In our Catholic faith, Confession provides relief and

compassion, forgiveness and freedom. St. Augustine called the confessional the medicine box. Noted psychologists understand the psychological benefits of the Sacrament of Reconciliation. God knows our sins. The sacramental graces of the confessional help us to take responsibility for our sins and heal our souls.

Again, today's battle starts with the mind. Our mind in modern society has been compromised. We must begin a dedicated process of recovery.

In order to begin a process of recovery, we must accept the need to recover. Our beautiful minds were meant to be filled with God's creation and with God's love for us and for others. Our minds were meant to be used for good things. We are here on earth to learn about love and practice love. If we are to become holy, and we desire this honestly, then why would we be open to watching others, through entertainment, behave in unholy ways? Is the truth that we have separated spirituality from daily life? In other words, we understand that we should work on holiness but we isolate that work to certain areas of our activity?

Thoughtful men and women of God will absorb the study of things divine and allow this study to permeate their entire days. A thoughtful man or woman of God takes his morning prayer and presses it into the day. In the middle of the day, a thoughtful man or woman of God stops and returns to his soul, wherein he finds God, and he then draws down again the truth about God and the truth about himself and returns to the remaining hours with renewed conviction.

The morning conviction is important, hence, at bare minimum, we recite the Allegiance Prayer and the prayer to Our Lady, Queen of the Church.

Imagine beginning a journey to an unknown destination in your car. Most people nowadays would set their Global Positioning System (GPS). If they were in a tearing hurry, perhaps they would just depart and then try to set the GPS en-route. This would be ill-advised and the reader is thinking, correctly, in terms of cars and highways, it may even be illegal to program a device while driving. We know it is dangerous!

Beginning the day without prayer is similar. We may have a general idea where we would like to go spiritually in a day but one thing we all know is that each day can throw us detours. The best we can do is resolve with God each morning that we will remain connected to Him so that He can direct us accurately in every moment.

Speaking of our morning contemplative prayer, we imagine our soul to be, not only our life's workshop, but God's workshop, too. God's kingdom coming through us is often dependent on our commitment to prayer time.

There are different areas to work on in each life. We must try to picture our life and imagine, using our mind, these areas delineated clearly.

In other words, imagine rooms in our soul where we will find our answers with Jesus. We will also find our mind's recovery.

Perhaps we can imagine a whole structure in our soul. The structure is shaped like a simple, traditional cross. We, in our humanity, can think of ourselves existing on earth where the two beams cross. We then retreat from our active experience of life into our souls to meet God. Our life on earth is where we suffer and this, the place where Christ hung, is also a reason to seek solace through prayer. This is Ground Zero for us who seek to become holy, the place where we go to encounter God in our soul, the point of meeting in the quest for a Trinitarian existence.

We, using our formula, present ourselves to Jesus and look up toward the first area that is, toward the top of the cross. We might designate this area as the area where we direct contemplative prayer. There we can experience profound intimacy with Christ. We acknowledge, we praise, we worship, we thank, we commit and we say our Allegiance Prayer (vocal prayer).

For the purposes of this structure, we are located, as stated, in the area of the cross where the body of Christ hung. This is significant. In our suffering humanity we resemble Christ crucified and it is with Him and from His heart that we both acknowledge the Father and pledge our allegiance to Him. The Holy Spirit, bursting from the heart of Christ compellingly to the Father, also bursts from us, even while we remain in our humanity.

My friends, regardless of our condition, regardless of our past failures, if we are in this place today at all, meaning, trying to pray, then we are working to some degree from within the Sacred Heart, from within the Divine Mercy, connected to the King, a reality which not only heals us but sends us out in a divinely meaningful way.

We must never be overly impressed by the sins we commit, even though we take our propensity to sin seriously. We should, instead, marvel at the possible life God will create for us if continue on with Him.

On either side of the cross, that is, where the arms of Christ were pinned, we have vocal prayer to our left and meditation prayer, or what we might think of as learning prayer, to the right. To repeat, contemplative prayer is straight up at the top of the cross. These three types of prayer comprise our active participation in relationship vertically with the Trinity.

We can think of prayer, in general, as our response to Love. If someone says to us, "I love you," we, when that love is authentic and unconditional, often instinctively respond in kind with our own "I love you, too." These three types of prayer constitute our own "I love you, too," to the Trinity. But these are the beginning of our answer to God's love. The Trinity must be allowed to move freely through our human existence and saturate it, so to speak. For the purpose of this treatment, we reference the lower portion of the cross, where we allow, through serious contemplation, the Trinity to impact, direct and transform our experience and actions, indeed, our whole participation in life on earth.

This Trinitarian existence, while we remain on earth, is a very busy existence. There is great work to be done. Hence the areas down either side of the lower part of the Cross. We are using our minds now, to imagine these rooms in our soul as a workshop where we do our divine work while we remain on earth.

Now we imagine the portion of the cross below the cross beams. This extends vertically all the way down to the ground. Picture yourself walking down a corridor as you make your way from the intersecting point of the cross. On either side of the corridor, there are rooms, each dedicated to specific contemplative prayer work which you can do with Jesus. In this way, we enable dynamic collaboration between self and Divine.

We will name both the rooms and the work to be done in the

rooms for the sake of clarity.

Let us call this corridor the Corridor of the Divine Will because we go up and down it with Christ, visiting the rooms to the left and right.

Conscience

The first room we encounter is on the left. This room is the room where we each, with Jesus, go to examine our conscience. This is a particular job and this room is best visited daily, at least for a brief look. That way there is no build up, which can be imagined as having a terribly stuffed closet where nothing can be found readily. When a closet is overly full and unexplored, disorganized and abandoned, one tends to walk past it quickly, with feelings of dread building up and guilt steadily siphoning joy from our days, even though one can be largely unaware, through denial, of this sad state of affairs.

Yes, the daily examination of conscience, quick though it may be, keeps one from storing big things and accumulating smaller things which do take up space.

Before making one's confession, this would be a room for a longer visit and if one is coming back to the sacraments after a long period of time, this room will hold necessary truth and relief but generally, one should *not* spend all of one's prayer time in this room. I would like to repeat that statement but perhaps the reader would find that tedious. Perhaps my desire, stated, to repeat the statement will prompt the reader to ask himself why I feel it is important. Use the formula for self-examination which connects the sin to the humanity and move on!

And remember that this place is but one room in the soul and that this work must be done distinctly. Jesus is with us in every part of our soul. We remember that HE wants to be the busy one, helping us, directing us and consoling us. Jesus desires to be our primary spiritual director.

There are other rooms and we will describe them in turn because it is very necessary that we become familiar with this structure so that we can recover and then order our minds as Jesus desires. And in this time of mind pollution, where our minds are disorganized and, let's admit, impulsive, we desire to place a temporary, heavenly ordered framework. When we are finished and our minds are purified and our contemplative work is effortlessly engaged in, we can lift the structure and there will be blissful order in our souls.

For now, we set about facilitating that order.

Relationships

The first room on the left of the cross, set aside for examination of conscience, is above another room, set aside for relationships. Scripture reminds us that others will know we are Christians by our love and it must be true that in this passage Scripture is not referring to our love for our cars or for our clothes and furniture. Scripture is referring to our love for God and for other people. Hence, the need to spend time with Jesus devoted solely to relationships.

In this room, it is helpful to allow Jesus to show us the people in our lives. So perhaps we might consider pictures of those important to us hanging on the walls. We are directed to whichever picture Jesus brings to our attention and we then contemplate that person with Him. There is no doubt whatsoever that Jesus loves each of these people without limit. And viewed from the eyes of the Savior, the situations we experience can look differently than when viewed simply from our own human eyes.

In a basic way, we must consider each of the important relationships in our lives with Christ each day and look for our duty. What action does our duty dictate for us in each of our primary relationships?

Spouses, for example, should remember that their spouse is the primary relationship in life. Each day, we must contemplate our spouse with Jesus, however briefly, and look for our duty to that person. Husbands and wives, remember, 'Spouse first, then children.' That is the order and that is the correct order to insulate a family from the ravages of divorce. And each parent should be, however briefly, contemplating each child, also, and asking Jesus which actions He would like for us to complete in each day. And then out further into our 'circles of service'. For a more complete treatment of 'circles of service' see *Serving in Clarity.*

For broader consideration in this room, we all remember being hurt. We all remember having a hard time overcoming certain hurts. Perhaps if we look at every person around us and remember that not only have they been hurt, but possibly hurt by us, we will be most appropriately disposed to rest into the relationships. Even the most loving relationships on earth are imperfect, after all.

Sometimes we are pitifully innocent victims and in those very real circumstances, we must acknowledge our innocence to ourselves and remember the Beautiful Victim who hung from the cross for three hours so that we could experience redemption. How He adores and heals those who suffer innocently.

"They're behaving terribly," we sometimes exclaim. People do behave badly. We, each of us, certainly behaves badly at times, therefore, it is not stunning that the people in our lives would make mistakes, too. What is important in this room of OUR soul is that we view the situations with Christ and determine our responses to each person from that Vertical Relationship we have committed to.

So…we see that there are some relationships which are easy and some which are more difficult. We need, in some cases, to move down the cross to another, third room on that side which is the Forgiveness Room.

Forgiveness

Picture yourself taking the picture of the person who has hurt you down from the wall in the Relationships Room and carrying it further down the corridor to the Forgiveness Room. Sometimes, we cry painful tears as we make the trek down the hall with the picture of one who hurt us. There, their image will hang, on that wall in the Forgiveness Room, until, with Christ, we are able to be healed enough to forgive this offender. In this room we understand that God gives us a special grace to forgive those who have hurt us but forgiveness can be a process as opposed to an event. When we find it difficult or impossible to forgive, we can rest in this room and be at peace during that process of finding forgiveness. This is a whole work unto itself and it is very important.

There are times when we are injured by someone in such a way that the injury creates for us an experience of trauma. In these cases, recovery will require a process, possibly even after we have forgiven. We must accept this and be understanding of ourselves as God is understanding of us. The following description of trauma, taken from the book *Ireland: Healing the Soul Wound*, by Margaret McGahon, will help us to separate out those experiences that are less straightforward than simply forgiving another person.

The internal emotional experience of trauma or re-stimulated trauma will usually involve:

- A sense of either shock, terror, horror, betrayal, humiliation, or shame

- Feelings of having no control or being powerless

- Feelings of being unprepared or without adequate resources to handle the situation

- A sense that one is not the same after, one is permanently different, scarred or damaged

- Feelings of alienation as a result-alone or trapped with the experience or feelings

In circumstances where we are traumatized, we recognize that for whatever reasons, we were extremely vulnerable and we were injured in a significant fashion. This is important to acknowledge.

Often, healing will involve talking this over with another person.

For now, let us return to the room of Relationships.

If we consider each person in our lives with Christ we can then decide, with Him, how we should love each person in this day. This is 'Work of the Day' and this is so important that it takes place in another room altogether, across the hall on the other side of the cross. Again, without consideration, our relationships will be vulnerable to our misfires. Our own image is quite possibly hanging on the wall of someone else's Forgiveness Room. It's best to determine what God wants from us for the people around us.

Why are there separate rooms for Relationships and Work of the Day? Because in the Relationships Room we study the relationships in an overall way. Am I influencing this person positively? Meeting my obligations to him or her? Am I being influenced against holiness by this person? Is this relationship one I should maintain or perhaps is it time to end it? Do I have a divine obligation to this person and if so what does that comprise overall? Am I meeting the hopes God has for us together if we are involved in a 'circle of service'? Is it possible to salvage a suffering relationship and if so how? Am I tempted against this person, rationally or irrationally? Why?

Work of the Day

In the Work of the Day room, we examine what, if anything, this person requires from us today and what, if anything, is our duty toward this person on this day. Mothers, Fathers, children, siblings, close friends, teachers, priests, religious, colleagues… we must all look each day at what God, Himself wants from us in each of our relationships. This can take all of two minutes each day. But if one makes this a habit, one will allow Jesus to show us the hopes and goals He wishes to achieve through us in the day.

With immediate family members, it might seem obvious, but it is not always as obvious as it needs to be and it is in these close relationships where we make the most mistakes and act from our wounds, all the while justifying casual or even bad behaviors. An old saying goes 'Familiarity breeds contempt.' While this is possibly true of some, it should never be true of the King's followers. Followers of the Returning King should abide by the saying, 'Familiarity breeds exquisite reverence'.

Therefore, if we, with Christ, examine each relationship calmly and contemplatively, with a sincere desire to hit the loving mark, Jesus will give us right inspirations and also directions.

And regarding directions, the Volumes are littered with them. We must not abandon the Volumes because God intended them, after Scripture, to be our holiness reference books. We must study them daily while we study God in this time of mind pollution. Lay apostles, the Volumes are a sublime gift to the times and if we read them like the latest fiction novel, we will dreadfully disappoint Jesus. Also, we are reading at a different level and different place each day, so the grace will remain fresh even as our own condition and circumstances change.

Back to business, when we are in the room of Relationships we remember that we are next to the room where we examine our conscience and that will give us humility and ongoing purpose of amendment with regard to our relationships. God is love and love is meant to be received and shared. Relationships are important to God and so we must work hard at relating as if we were already saints in heaven.

My friends, on the way into the room of Relationships, perhaps we could imagine something like an umbrella stand outside the door. In it there are signs, not umbrellas. Each of us must take one into this room so that we will be armed with the greatest possible amount of truth. The sign we pick up and carry into this room says, "I AM IMPERFECT." When we look at others with Jesus, we feel the weight of this sign and it reminds us that not only are others carrying similar signs, but others are feeling the weight of our mistakes. Our imperfection can delight those who love us if they truly love us but it can also wound them. An awareness of this with the commensurate humility protects everyone and we need protection badly in this time of embarrassing self-righteousness and victim identities.

Yes, sometimes the truth about our imperfection accompanies us everywhere but into our own awareness. How often do we complain about the imperfection of those around us while ignoring our own? But those days are over for us, dear lay apostles. We are doing the hard work in our souls using our minds. We are using our minds and do so to the accompaniment of the truth of our fallen natures, yes, but also accompanied by an enormous awareness of God's mercy and grace.

Across the corridor we have three more rooms. One is a very important room where we identify and store the things that can otherwise clutter the hallways, distract us from our work and disturb our peace. It is the room for Temptations.

Temptations

Ah...temptations. They swirl, seduce, cajole, justify, distract, dig in, lock out, sadden, crush, confuse and ultimately, sanctify. What? Sanctify? My friends, we must be adult about temptations. Where would we be without them? In denial, of course. Temptations are a part of our faith life just as virtue is a part of our faith life.

Picture a professional swimmer. The professional swimmer is very attentive to pushing hard off the side of the pool when he makes his turn at the end of the lap. Why? Because the harder he pushes, the greater the force which propels him away from that side and into the next lap toward the other side.

We must view our temptations this way, and indeed, even our sins.

My friends, having a room for our temptations will help us in many ways. Once we identify something as a temptation and we place it in its proper location in our soul, we, in a sense, have declared open war on our fallen nature. Placing something in the room called Temptations is like saying, "No more pretending. This is not worthy thinking and it is not going to prompt worthy action, suitable to one who stands beneath the cross of the crushed and crucified Savior." Remember, dear apostles, we stand at the foot of the cross alongside Saint John and Our Lady, the Queen of the Church. We can justify bad or childish behavior, and we do, but interiorly, here in our orderly soul, we know that God hopes for a good response to His love and grace.

The thoughtful man or woman of God is able to say, "This desire is a bad desire and could result in a sinful action." My friends, walk it firmly down the hall and deposit it in the room with the other bad desires. When you enter that room, Jesus is there. If you hand him the bad desire, He will know what to do with it. Leave it with him, walk out calmly, carrying the Lord's gift of Big Trust. Then, bolt down the corridor to the Work of the Day Room. In that room you will always find a worthy action to distract yourself from the more unworthy actions which are being prompted by the bad desires.

The fallen nature is a reality but it is not something we should use to produce a stream of excuses. The fallen nature should be viewed like the wall of the pool which we push hard against to propel ourselves toward the other side of the pool, the virtues. We can work on the virtues by spending time in the room of the Characteristics of the Divine Will.

Now, there are thoughts and desires which tempt one into sinful actions and there are thoughts and desires which tempt one into sinful dispositions. Let's call them dispositions of pride, arrogance, entitlement, rebellion, defiance, aggression, lust, anger, bitterness, hopelessness, unwillingness to serve, selfishness, sneering envy, jealousy, greed, falseness, recklessness, and, to allow one to stand alone, superiority toward rightful authority. That one should be in the Temptation Room turning slowly around with hateful fluorescent lights bathing it in all its cruel destructiveness, disobedience.

How many holy projects and good works were sacrificed at the anti-altar where this temptation sits? How many vocations? How many of God's hopes? Those offering homage to this anti-altar will always be harboring a bundle of these other dispositions. It does not matter which dispositions brought us here. The outcome is the same. God's plans for a particular contribution from us must be thrown unto the burning pyre of temptation against the rightful authority if we give in to these dispositions. Let us each take note and remember the truth so we cannot change it through clever arguments or slick justifications.

My friends, if we can order our minds with Jesus, giving this holy work the time it requires and deserves, we will be safer. For example, if we acknowledge our pain at being wounded, by placing others in the Forgiveness Room, we will insulate God's plan for us and God's plan for others. We will learn to retain our joy in the most ridiculous of negative circumstances. We are being fashioned as arrows in the quiver of Renewal. We must submit to the formation of the Returning King by spending time working in this structure of holiness in our souls. A thoughtful man or woman of God craves this time and comes to move quickly and efficiently up and down the Corridor of the Divine Will, fully embracing the Trinitarian existence that is, as stated, God's greatest hope for each of His children.

Characteristics of the Divine Will

We, to best achieve the correct dispositions, visit the room where we study the Characteristics of the Divine Will, which we can also attribute to the Father, Son and the Holy Spirit, that is, the Trinity. We have identified these characteristics as Gentleness, Kindness, Generosity of Heart, Truthfulness, Eagerness to Serve, Prudence and Humility. If we take them, first together in a superficial way, repeating them to ourselves at least once each day, then we will impress them upon our minds and gain the ability to access them in our reciprocal expression of love, meaning our prayer, Verbal, Meditative and Contemplative. And these characteristics will be accessible to us also in the other rooms. How helpful it will be for us to consider these characteristics when we are in the room of the Conscience. Clearly, we should consider these characteristics in the Relationships Room and of course we will need to remember how to consider those who have hurt us in the Forgiveness Room. In the Temptation Room we will have something of a contrast if we bring these characteristics with us. And we definitely want them prevalent in the Work of the Day Room because working with these characteristics helps us to most accurately reflect God.

We remember that God always interacts with us according to these characteristics and if we display these words in the room of Courage and Consolation, we will remember the times when we succeeded in behaving in the manner in which Jesus behaved. We will possess them all with patience, my friends, so let us have courage and begin by learning them by heart as a child learns his arithmetic tables.

Gentleness, kindness, generosity of heart, truthfulness, eagerness to serve, humility and prudence.

If one attends a university for a full degree course, one becomes familiar with the hallways, nooks and crannies of the campus. So, too, must we become familiar with this deeply personal place where we seek union with God. Let us picture the Corridor of the Divine Will as a familiar place for us. We move back and forth from room to room, doing the hard work as we fight the good fight. We pray for strength, study the examples in Scripture and ultimately bring everything into active and dynamic contemplative prayer.

Far from being isolated in this process of becoming, we are enveloped in the Holy Spirit who directs, confides, refreshes and protects. Truly, it is the Holy Spirit who draws, enlightens, unites, blends and bonds us further and further into the Trinitarian existence. We must remember each day that we are beings created by God for eternity. That is not something we choose, by the way. We were created by God and we were created for eternity. There WILL be an afterlife. Because someone denies the existence of God does not mean that person will not be face to face with the same God we proclaim upon their death.

To be even more clear, claiming that God does not exist, will in no way impact the existence of God.

This truth would merit close examination by those proclaiming atheism and by those passing atheistic beliefs to their children. One would go so far as to encourage a person to prove that God did not exist before one dared to make the claim that God does not exist.

Picture a person standing in front of a tree. "This tree does not exist," the person states confidently.

This is how some of us view atheists. Best to look at the person and try to understand his or her pain in that experience of blindness.

A concern would be, though, that the person who denies the existence of God is denying his spiritual vision or supernatural sense but perhaps the person is temporarily numbed to spiritual realities. So be it. Many who claim atheism practice morality with zeal and sacrifice. God will be so grateful to them for their example of service.

For us, we believe in the Trinity and strive for the Trinitarian existence. Let us do so now with everything we have learned in this time and view ourselves as enjoying the active tutoring by the Returning King Himself.

Blessed are those who have not seen and who not only believe but have the courage to proclaim God!

At the bottom of the cross we reference the beautiful, broad room which consumes the whole base. It is an important room and we will need it very often. Many people experience life changing moments in this room and we are sometimes surprised to find ourselves in it in delightfully unexpected moments. Sometimes we come to this room in sheer desperation and sometimes we are brought by the Spirit with generosity that humbles us completely. Sometimes we feel we are lying in a heap outside of this doorway, unable to enter.

This is the room of Consolation and Courage.

Consolation and Courage

My friends, we know that we are loved by God. He created us, in love, contemplating us tenderly into existence. But sometimes, given all that occurs in life, we have difficulty accepting that we are lovable. This doubt can bring people to all manner of substitute love experiences and addictions. Craving love from each other is natural. God Himself craves love from humanity. As we were created in His image and likeness, it follows that we would also crave love. We must rest in this room and revel in the true love God has for us personally. Only in this way will we be able to detect true love and then come to identify it accurately in the world.

For example, when we rest in the room of Courage and Consolation, we will find ourselves free to be unguarded and honest. We will feel totally ourselves, with both our virtue and our sin. Arguably, we will only truly come to know ourselves here. We will have a clear understanding of our dignity and my friends, in this time of ungodly behaviors which strip dignity, we need to have a good working understanding of what being dignified feels like. We can then carry that feeling of dignity into the world and when our dignity is at risk, either by a group of people or by a pattern of behavior, we will be so nicely steeped in our holy dignity that we will immediately recognize any departure from it or any threat to it.

Remember, a deep spiritual experience is actually just an experience of connection. Should we qualify connection? Think of an electric cord being plugged in. Hopefully, there is no explosion. What we want is the current to be transported from the source into and through the cord. That's all. That's all that is needed. The recipient of the connection experiences something like a knowing, a light. A recipient of divine connection knows God is real and knows God loves him. This alone, in whatever form it takes for the individual, can create the most absurd amount of courage and can give one consolation enough to persevere even in ridiculous difficulty.

My friends, if you follow this Contemplative Prayer formula and investigate your life and service within this structure, God will make Himself known to you and you will ideally gain order in your soul and prayer life. One should seek, through this determined work, greater truth about oneself and greater clarity about one's intended service in each day.

As a warning, those seeking mystical experiences for sensational gratification will most seldom be granted them.

But how does one discern mystical experiences? This is a very real dilemma for some, particularly for those who spend most of their time considering the enemy.

In short, when God acts in the life of a soul, there comes deep peace, quiet consolation, clear direction and humility. What is humility? One holy man said that humility is simply knowing one's place. If we know our place, we are liberated. We seek only to serve calmly and faithfully.

Those who consider God's enemy with equal or even greater attention than they consider God are prone to make claims of a mystical nature and this places them in danger. Additionally, this gives very bad example to others who may not be distracted by these studies and practices of darkness. May God bless these words and grant that the words prompt clarity through the Spirit.

My friends in Christ Jesus, whom do we follow? Clearly, we aim to follow Jesus Christ, the son of Mary. How on earth can we make this claim if all we talk about is the one to be crushed under Mary's heel?

This has to be very clear so I will paint a picture. Imagine a gymnast who is destined to compete in the Olympics. The coach is there, waiting to work. The Olympic hopeful wanders outside, into the alley behind the gym. There she studies the bad behaviors of those who mock her coach. They are breaking windows, scrawling graffiti on walls and assaulting other people. They lure people away from their work, all the while jeering and sneering at anyone who trains for the Olympics. The Coach waits and waits but all the gymnast seems interested in is watching and talking about those who have rejected meaningful sport.

Remember, please. Evil is pitifully limited. It can have no action against heaven except to try to draw you away from it. Goodness is unlimited, infinite in its ramifications.

Your decisions today affect you and others eternally. Your decisions today affect you and others eternally. Your decisions today affect you and others eternally.

"Oh dear," you might be saying, "The writer is definitely repeating herself now." It's true. I am. I am repeating myself because if you do not do this work in your soul each day, God's kingdom will not be able to come fully through you. It is that simple.

The world is in an emergency situation. (It always is if you are following Christ.) God has orchestrated a Rescue Mission. We are chosen to help Him. He, to some degree, has entrusted the Gospel message to you today. What you do today affects those around you and the whole world. Your decisions, if made without contemplative prayer, will be questionable. Bad decisions, even small ones, can set into motion negative chains of events which damage our loved ones and send out bad ripple effects. But that is not what we should think about. We should be thinking with the most consoling and absorbing wonder at what good ripple effects can originate from us on each day!

Lay apostles, let us apply ourselves. If the Lord has given us the faculties to do this work it must mean that He desires it.

With regard to discernment, please know that a real connection with God will prompt a peaceful increase in the Characteristics of the Divine Will. A real connection with God will prompt humility, for example, as opposed to arrogance and anger. A real connection with God will prompt gentleness and eagerness to serve. If one is claiming a healthy prayer life but one is unwilling to see to one's duties of the day, can we really find that credible? I do not think so and many non-followers have been badly stung by those claiming a prayer life which does not play out in action.

Truly, the cruelty of falseness rocks even the staunchest of us who believe. Good discernment will prompt prudent decisions as opposed to reckless and dramatic actions. Prudence stands the test of time and while others do not always find it exciting, the prudent decision will insulate and protect, not just for today but for the future.

Kindness is a fruit of a good prayer life, as is generosity of heart. To be clear, generosity of heart produces kindness and those disposed this way focus on the potential and the good qualities of those around them instead of searching for flaws to inflate, distort, exploit and proclaim. These characteristics will be identifiable in the one who is experiencing real connection with God.

My friends, perhaps we should spend a little more time on the Forgiveness Room. It is clear that people are vulnerable to mistakes in life and people are also vulnerable to being wounded by the mistakes of those around them. We all need this room. And we can be in any of the other rooms and find out that there is someone whose picture we need to take off the wall and carry down the Corridor of the Divine Will for a period of time and concerted effort in the Forgiveness Room.

What should happen here? Truly, Jesus is the Master of this whole structure for you and through the power of the Holy Spirit, with Christ as the guide, you will proceed into forgiveness of others. How? One can imagine that as one peruses the images hanging in one's room of Forgiveness, one will study the countenances of others with Christ.

Hmm. How does Jesus view these people? Well, He views them in totality, meaning, He understands that the whole of their life experience has contributed to their decisions on each day. Jesus will know their full truth. We, of course, do not. Most of what we do when we evaluate others is speculate and guess. Jesus, on the other hand, sees exactly how badly these individuals have been hurt by others. We do not have access to their private anguishes. Only Jesus can see clearly the level of malice which caused them to act out against us. Perhaps Jesus will help us to see that there are understandable reasons for the actions, both good and bad, of others. Possibly, in the company of Christ, we will be able to see how much good a person has been able to produce, despite their wounds and despite the bad actions they committed against us. Remember, nobody knows anyone else's full story.

My friends, if we were terribly hurt by others, perhaps we hang their picture in this room and just look at Jesus as HE studies them. Maybe that is the way to start in cases where we are afraid we cannot forgive or that we do not *want* to forgive. That is true at times. We might be afraid that if we forgive someone we will become vulnerable again.

And we must admit that it can be easier to hang on to a grudge than to release it. We have to admit that we wish we had not been vulnerable. It is true. We can despise our vulnerability and feel shame around it. We can be angry at ourselves that we craved love from someone who hurt us or that we trusted someone and they betrayed our trust. Did we crave acceptance? Perfect love? Should we learn to crave acceptance and perfect love from only God? Because if we can get to that point, we will be free. God does accept us. God does love us perfectly. We must learn to accept imperfection in ourselves and also imperfection in others.

Often it is unrealistic expectation which can cause us such pain. Also, one suspects that unrealistic expectation sometimes impedes our ability to forgive. Others were imperfect, they hurt us and we must grieve. Sorrow must be expressed, dear friends. The shortest verse of Scripture is from John 11:35. "Jesus wept." So it is good that He keeps us company in this room, and indeed, in every room.

And if we look closely in this room, we may see our own picture hanging on the wall. This is huge! It may be that we have to forgive ourselves before we are ready to forgive others. Oh dear. We have landed in a truth. Self-hatred belongs in the Temptation Room, ultimately, but we have to start here, in the Forgiveness Room.

Lay apostle, picture yourself walking down the Corridor and into the Forgiveness Room. You are carrying a big picture of yourself. Hang it on the wall. Look squarely at the image of yourself and say right now, "Self, I forgive you for being imperfect, yesterday, today and tomorrow. Self, it's true. God forgives you and I forgive you, too!"

How did I leave that this long? Truly, I must forgive myself for not putting that in the first paragraph but all is well that ends well.

On a final note, please do not think there is a day when you should skip the Temptation Room. You should not. Try to stop in on the way to the Work of the Day Room and have a look at where you might get tripped up. Feeling overwhelmed? Inadequate? Is this from God? If you walk quickly past this room it could be like walking past the overstuffed closet. We can generally assume some small bit of temptation is active in the day.

We can be tempted to act in ways that are unholy or we can be tempted to omit duties which are rightfully ours. We can be tempted to make judgments on others which are over and above a calm evaluation of actions taken against us. We can believe we know it all or that we know better than the rightful authority. And, there will be times when we do know more than those around us or when the rightful authority gets it wrong. This room will be very necessary to us at that point because we will want to tread gingerly, indeed, at those times.

We use this room, generally, to help us avoid sin, which the Catechism says "…wounds man's nature and injures solidarity" (CCC 1872). Unity is crucial. And it will present us each with an 'ask', sometimes a big 'ask'.

We must keep away from denial insofar as we are able.

Consider denial a little alcove in the Temptation Room. It has pictures of us on the wall pretending to be holy. Perhaps we have hung images of ourselves doing overtly holy things so that we can be distracted from the not so holy inclinations and actions we are harboring and trying to ignore.

Again, have a look. Maybe it is not a problem but this alcove merits a glimpse now and then.

Additionally, the Courage and Consolation Room will look different for everyone just as everyone's soul looks different. And we are right to share with others those things which comforted us. Scripture urges us to do so.

We will all have different verses of Scripture in our rooms but one which might stand out is from Philippians, 4:13. "I can do all things through Christ who strengthens me."

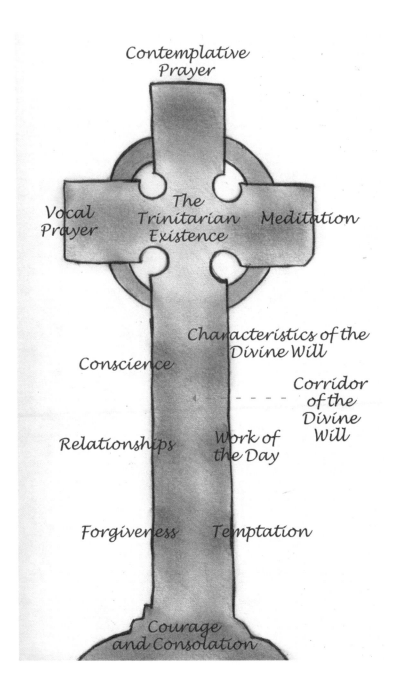

Appendix

Guidelines for Lay Apostles

As lay apostles of Jesus Christ the Returning King, we agree to perform our basic obligations as practicing Catholics. Additionally, we will adopt the following spiritual practices, as best we can:

1. **Allegiance Prayer** and **Morning Offering**, plus a brief prayer for the Holy Father
2. **Eucharistic Adoration**, one hour per week
3. **Prayer Group Participation**, monthly, at which we pray the Luminous Mysteries of the Holy Rosary and read the Monthly Message
4. **Monthly Confession**
5. Further, we will follow the example of Jesus Christ as set out in the Holy Scripture, treating all others with His patience and kindness.

Allegiance Prayer

Dear God in Heaven, I pledge my allegiance to You. I give You my life, my work and my heart. In turn, give me the grace of obeying Your every direction to the fullest possible extent. Amen.

Morning Offering

O Jesus, through the Immaculate Heart of Mary, I offer You the prayers, works, joys and sufferings of this day, for all the intentions of Your Sacred Heart, in union with the Holy Sacrifice of the Mass throughout the world, in reparation for my sins, and for the intentions of the Holy Father. Amen.

Prayer for the Holy Father

Our Lady Queen of the Church, protect our Holy Father, Francis, and bless his intentions.

Promise from Jesus to His Lay Apostles

May 12, 2005

Your message to souls remains constant. Welcome each soul to the rescue mission. You may assure each lay apostle that just as they concern themselves with My interests, I will concern Myself with theirs. They will be placed in My Sacred Heart and I will defend and protect them. I will also pursue complete conversion of each of their loved ones. So you see, the souls who serve in this rescue mission as My beloved lay apostles will know peace. The world cannot make this promise as only Heaven can bestow peace on a soul. This is truly Heaven's mission and I call every one of Heaven's children to assist Me. You will be well rewarded, My dear ones.

What about the Monthly Prayer Group?

Jesus asks us to form lay apostle prayer groups. He asks us to meet once each month to pray the Luminous Mysteries of the Holy Rosary and read the Monthly Message. A prayer group can be as small as two people within a family or as large as hundreds in a church.

Five Luminous Mysteries:

1. The Baptism of Jesus
2. The Wedding at Cana
3. The Proclamation of the Kingdom of God
4. The Transfiguration
5. The Institution of the Eucharist

Monthly Messages

For seven years Jesus gave Anne a message for the world on the first day of every month. Each month the apostolate reads and contemplates one of these monthly messages.

To receive the monthly messages you may access our website at **www.directionforourtimes.org** or call us at one of our offices to be placed on our mailing list.

We have also printed a book which contains all of the monthly messages. It can be purchased through our website as well.

Prayers Taken from The Volumes

Prayers to God the Father

"I trust You, God. I offer You my pain in the spirit of acceptance and I will serve You in every circumstance."

"God my Father in Heaven, You are all mercy. You love me and see my every sin. God, I call on You now as the Merciful Father. Forgive my every sin. Wash away the stains on my soul so that I may once again rest in complete innocence. I trust You, Father in Heaven. I rely on You. I thank You. Amen."

"God my Father, calm my spirit and direct my path."

"God, I have made mistakes. I am sorry. I am Your child, though, and seek to be united to You."

"I believe in God. I believe Jesus is calling me. I believe my Blessed Mother has requested my help. Therefore I am going to pray on this day and every day."

"God my Father, help me to understand."

Prayers to Jesus

"Jesus, I give You my day."

"Jesus, how do You want to use me on this day? You have a willing servant in me, Jesus. Allow me to work for the Kingdom."

"Lord, what can I do today to prepare for Your coming? Direct me, Lord, and I will see to Your wishes."

"Lord, help me."

"Jesus, love me."

Prayers to the Angels

"Angels from Heaven, direct my path."

"Dearest angel guardian, I desire to serve Jesus by remaining at peace. Please obtain for me the graces necessary to maintain His divine peace in my heart."

Prayers for a Struggling Soul

"Jesus, what do You think of all this? Jesus, what do You want me to do for this soul? Jesus, show me how to bring You into this situation."

"Angel guardian, thank you for your constant vigil over this soul. Saints in Heaven, please assist this dear angel."

Prayers for Children

"God in Heaven, You are the Creator of all things. Please send Your graces down upon our world."

"Jesus, I love You."

"Jesus, I trust in You. Jesus, I trust in You. Jesus, I trust in You."

"Jesus, I offer You my day."

"Mother Mary, help me to be good."

How to Recite the Chaplet of Divine Mercy

The Chaplet of Mercy is recited using ordinary Rosary beads of five decades. The Chaplet is preceded by two opening prayers from the *Diary* of Saint Faustina and followed by a closing prayer.

1. Make the Sign of the Cross

In the name of the Father, and of the Son, and of the Holy Spirit. Amen.

2. Optional Opening Prayers

You expired, Jesus, but the source of life gushed forth for souls, and the ocean of mercy opened up for the whole world. O Fount of Life, unfathomable Divine Mercy, envelop the whole world and empty Yourself out upon us.

O Blood and Water, which gushed forth from the Heart of Jesus as a fountain of mercy for us, I trust in You!

3. Our Father

Our Father, who art in Heaven, hallowed be Thy name. Thy Kingdom come. Thy will be done on earth as it is in Heaven. Give us this day our daily bread. And forgive us our trespasses, as we forgive those who trespass against us. And lead us not into temptation, but deliver us from evil. Amen.

4. Hail Mary

Hail Mary, full of grace, the Lord is with thee. Blessed art thou among women, and blessed is the fruit of thy womb, Jesus. Holy Mary, Mother of God, pray for us sinners, now and at the hour of our death. Amen.

5. The Apostles' Creed

I believe in God, the Father Almighty, Creator of Heaven and earth. I believe in Jesus Christ, His only Son, Our Lord. He was conceived by the power of the Holy Spirit and born of the Virgin Mary. He suffered under Pontius Pilate, was crucified, died, and was buried. He descended to the dead. On the third day He rose again. He ascended into Heaven, and is seated at the right hand of the Father. He will come again to judge the living and the dead. I believe in the Holy Spirit, the holy Catholic Church, the Communion of Saints, the forgiveness of sins, the resurrection of the body, and life everlasting. Amen.

6. The Eternal Father

Eternal Father, I offer You the Body and Blood, Soul and Divinity of Your Dearly Beloved Son, our Lord, Jesus Christ, in atonement for our sins and those of the whole world.

7. On the Ten Small Beads of Each Decade

For the sake of His Sorrowful Passion, have mercy on us and on the whole world.

8. Repeat for the remaining decades

Saying the "Eternal Father" (6) on the "Our Father" bead and then 10 "For the sake of His Sorrowful Passion" (7) on the following "Hail Mary" beads.

9. Conclude with Holy God

Holy God, Holy Mighty One, Holy Immortal One, have mercy on us and on the whole world.

10. Optional Closing Prayer

Eternal God, in whom mercy is endless and the treasury of compassion—inexhaustible, look kindly upon us and increase Your mercy in us, that in difficult moments we might not despair nor become despondent, but with great confidence submit ourselves to Your holy will, which is Love and Mercy itself.

To learn more about the image of The Divine Mercy, the Chaplet of Divine Mercy and the series of revelations given to St. Faustina Kowalska please contact:

Marians of the Immaculate Conception
Stockbridge, Massachusetts 01263
Telephone 800-462-7426
www.marian.org

How to Pray the Rosary

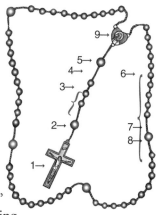

1. Make the Sign of the Cross and say the "Apostles Creed."
2. Say the "Our Father."
3. Say three "Hail Marys."
4. Say the "Glory be to the Father."
5. Announce the First Mystery; then say the "Our Father."
6. Say ten "Hail Marys," while meditating on the Mystery.
7. Say the "Glory be to the Father." After each decade say the following prayer requested by the Blessed Virgin Mary at Fatima: "O my Jesus, forgive us our sins, save us from the fires of hell, lead all souls to Heaven, especially those in most need of Thy mercy."
8. Announce the Second Mystery: then say the "Our Father." Repeat 6 and 7 and continue with the Third, Fourth, and Fifth Mysteries in the same manner.
9. Say the "Hail, Holy Queen" on the medal after the five decades are completed.

As a general rule, depending on the season, the Joyful Mysteries are said on Monday and Saturday; the Sorrowful Mysteries on Tuesday and Friday; the Glorious Mysteries on Wednesday and Sunday; and the Luminous Mysteries on Thursday.

Papal Reflections of the Mysteries

The Joyful Mysteries

The Joyful Mysteries are marked by the joy radiating from the event of the Incarnation. This is clear from the very first mystery, the Annunciation, where Gabriel's greeting to the Virgin of Nazareth is linked to an invitation to messianic joy: "Rejoice, Mary." The whole of salvation... had led up to this greeting.

(Prayed on Mondays and Saturdays, and optional on Sundays during Advent and the Christmas Season.)

The Luminous Mysteries

Moving on from the infancy and the hidden life in Nazareth to the public life of Jesus, our contemplation brings us to those mysteries which may be called in a special way "mysteries of light." Certainly, the whole mystery of Christ is a mystery of light. He is the "Light of the world" (John 8:12). Yet this truth emerges in a special way during the years of His public life. (Prayed on Thursdays.)

The Sorrowful Mysteries

The Gospels give great prominence to the Sorrowful Mysteries of Christ. From the beginning, Christian piety, especially during the Lenten devotion of the Way of the Cross, has focused on the individual moments of the Passion, realizing that here is found the culmination of the revelation of God's love and the source of our salvation. (Prayed on Tuesdays and Fridays, and optional on Sundays during Lent.)

The Glorious Mysteries

"The contemplation of Christ's face cannot stop at the image of the Crucified One. He is the Risen One!" The Rosary has always expressed this knowledge born of faith and invited the believer to pass beyond the darkness of the Passion in order to gaze upon Christ's glory in the Resurrection and Ascension... Mary herself would be raised to that same glory in the Assumption. (Prayed on Wednesdays and Sundays.)

From the *Apostolic Letter The Rosary of the Virgin Mary*, Pope John Paul II, Oct. 16, 2002.

Prayers of the Rosary

The Sign of the Cross
In the name of the Father, and of the Son, and of the Holy Spirit. Amen.

The Apostles' Creed
I believe in God, the Father Almighty, Creator of Heaven and earth. I believe in Jesus Christ, His only Son, Our Lord. He was conceived by the power of the Holy Spirit and born of the Virgin Mary. He suffered under Pontius Pilate, was crucified, died, and was buried. He descended to the dead. On the third day He rose again. He ascended into Heaven, and is seated at the right hand of the Father. He will come again to judge the living and the dead. I believe in the Holy Spirit, the holy Catholic Church, the Communion of Saints, the forgiveness of sins, the resurrection of the body, and life everlasting. Amen.

Our Father
Our Father, who art in Heaven, hallowed be Thy name. Thy Kingdom come. Thy will be done on earth as it is in Heaven. Give us this day our daily bread. And forgive us our trespasses, as we forgive those who trespass against us. And lead us not into temptation, but deliver us from evil. Amen.

Hail Mary
Hail Mary, full of grace, the Lord is with thee. Blessed art thou among women, and blessed is the fruit of thy womb, Jesus. Holy Mary, Mother of God, pray for us sinners, now and at the hour of our death. Amen.

Glory Be to the Father
Glory be to the Father, and to the Son, and to the Holy Spirit. As it was in the beginning, is now, and ever shall be, world without end. Amen.

Hail Holy Queen

Hail, Holy Queen, Mother of Mercy, our life, our sweetness and our hope. To thee do we cry, poor banished children of Eve. To thee do we send up our sighs, mourning and weeping in this valley of tears. Turn then, most gracious Advocate, thine eyes of mercy towards us. And after this, our exile, show unto us the blessed fruit of thy womb, Jesus. O clement, O loving, O sweet Virgin Mary!

Pray for us, O Holy Mother of God.
That we may be made worthy of the promises of Christ.

The Mysteries

First Joyful Mystery:
The Annunciation

And when the angel had come to her, he said, "Hail, full of grace, the Lord is with thee. Blessed art thou among women."

(*Luke* 1:28)

One *Our Father*, Ten *Hail Marys*,
One *Glory Be*, etc.

Fruit of the Mystery: ***Humility***

Second Joyful Mystery:
The Visitation

Elizabeth was filled with the Holy Spirit and cried out in a loud voice: "Blest are you among women and blest is the fruit of your womb."   (*Luke* 1:41-42)

One *Our Father*, Ten *Hail Marys*,
One *Glory Be*, etc.

Fruit of the Mystery: ***Love of Neighbor***

Third Joyful Mystery:
The Birth of Jesus

She gave birth to her first-born Son and wrapped Him in swaddling clothes and laid Him in a manger, because there was no room for them in the place where travelers lodged. (*Luke* 2:7)

One *Our Father*, Ten *Hail Marys*,
One *Glory Be*, etc.

Fruit of the Mystery: **Poverty**

Fourth Joyful Mystery:
The Presentation

When the day came to purify them according to the law of Moses, the couple brought Him up to Jerusalem so that He could be presented to the Lord, for it is written in the law of the Lord, "Every first-born male shall be consecrated to the Lord."
(*Luke* 2:22-23)

One *Our Father*, Ten *Hail Marys*,
One *Glory Be*, etc.

Fruit of the Mystery: **Obedience**

Fifth Joyful Mystery:
The Finding of the Child Jesus in the Temple

On the third day they came upon Him in the temple sitting in the midst of the teachers, listening to them and asking them questions. (*Luke* 2:46)

One *Our Father*, Ten *Hail Marys*,
One *Glory Be*, etc.

Fruit of the Mystery: **Joy in Finding Jesus**

First Luminous Mystery:
The Baptism of Jesus

And when Jesus was baptized… the heavens were opened and He saw the Spirit of God descending like a dove, and alighting on Him, and lo, a voice from Heaven, saying "this is My beloved Son," with whom I am well pleased." (*Matthew* 3:16-17)

One *Our Father*, Ten *Hail Marys*,
One *Glory Be*, etc.

Fruit of the Mystery: **Openness to the Holy Spirit**

Second Luminous Mystery:
The Wedding at Cana

His mother said to the servants, "Do whatever He tells you." . . . Jesus said to them, "Fill the jars with water." And they filled them up to the brim.

(John 2:5-7)

One Our Father, Ten Hail Marys,
One Glory Be, etc.

Fruit of the Mystery: ***To Jesus through Mary***

Third Luminous Mystery:
The Proclamation of the Kingdom of God

"And preach as you go, saying, 'The Kingdom of Heaven is at hand.' Heal the sick, raise the dead, cleanse lepers, cast out demons. You received without pay, give without pay."

(Matthew 10:7-8)

One Our Father, Ten Hail Marys,
One Glory Be, etc.

Fruit of the Mystery: ***Repentance and Trust in God***

Fourth Luminous Mystery:
The Transfiguration

And as He was praying, the appearance of His countenance was altered and His raiment become dazzling white. And a voice came out of the cloud saying, "This is My Son, My chosen; listen to Him!

(Luke 9:29, 35)

One Our Father, Ten Hail Marys,
One Glory Be, etc.

Fruit of the Mystery: ***Desire for Holiness***

Fifth Luminous Mystery:
The Institution of the Eucharist

And He took bread, and when He had given thanks He broke it and gave it to them, saying, "This is My body which is given for you." . . . And likewise the cup after supper, saying, "This cup which is poured out for you is the new covenant in My blood."

(Luke 22:19-20)

One Our Father, Ten Hail Marys,
One Glory Be, etc.

Fruit of the Mystery: ***Adoration***

First Sorrowful Mystery:
The Agony in the Garden

In His anguish He prayed with all the greater intensity, and His sweat became like drops of blood falling to the ground. Then He rose from prayer and came to His disciples, only to find them asleep, exhausted with grief. (Luke 22:44-45)

One Our Father, Ten Hail Marys,
One Glory Be, etc.

Fruit of the Mystery: ***Sorrow for Sin***

Second Sorrowful Mystery:
The Scourging at the Pillar

Pilate's next move was to take Jesus and have Him scourged.

(John 19:1)

One Our Father, Ten Hail Marys,
One Glory Be, etc.

Fruit of the Mystery: ***Purity***

Third Sorrowful Mystery:
The Crowning with Thorns

They stripped off His clothes and wrapped Him in a scarlet military cloak. Weaving a crown out of thorns they fixed it on His head, and stuck a reed in His right hand... (Matthew 27:28-29)

One Our Father, Ten Hail Marys,
One Glory Be, etc.

Fruit of the Mystery: ***Courage***

Fourth Sorrowful Mystery:
The Carrying of the Cross

… carrying the cross by Himself, He went out to what is called the Place of the Skull (in Hebrew, Golgotha).   (*John* 19:17)

One *Our Father*, Ten *Hail Marys*,
One *Glory Be*, etc.

Fruit of the Mystery: **Patience**

Fifth Sorrowful Mystery:
The Crucifixion

Jesus uttered a loud cry and said, "Father, into Your hands I commend My spirit." After He said this, He expired.   (*Luke* 23:46)

One *Our Father*, Ten *Hail Marys*,
One *Glory Be*, etc.

Fruit of the Mystery: **Perseverance**

First Glorious Mystery:
The Resurrection

You need not be amazed! You are looking for Jesus of Nazareth, the one who was crucified. He has been raised up; He is not here. See the place where they laid Him."   (*Mark* 16:6)

One *Our Father*, Ten *Hail Marys*,
One *Glory Be*, etc.

Fruit of the Mystery: **Faith**

Second Glorious Mystery:
The Ascension

Then, after speaking to them, the Lord Jesus was taken up into Heaven and took His seat at God's right hand.   (*Mark* 16:19)

One *Our Father*, Ten *Hail Marys*,
One *Glory Be*, etc.

Fruit of the Mystery: **Hope**

Third Glorious Mystery:
The Descent of the Holy Spirit

All were filled with the Holy Spirit. They began to express themselves in foreign tongues and make bold proclamation as the Spirit prompted them. (*Acts* 2:4)

One *Our Father*, Ten *Hail Marys*,
One *Glory Be*, etc.

Fruit of the Mystery: ***Love of God***

Fourth Glorious Mystery:
The Assumption

You are the glory of Jerusalem... you are the splendid boast of our people... God is pleased with what you have wrought. May you be blessed by the Lord Almighty forever and ever.

(*Judith* 15:9-10)

One *Our Father*, Ten *Hail Marys*,
One *Glory Be*, etc.

Fruit of the Mystery: ***Grace of a Happy Death***

Fifth Glorious Mystery:
The Coronation

A great sign appeared in the sky, a woman clothed with the sun, with the moon under her feet, and on her head a crown of twelve stars. (*Revelation* 12:1)

One *Our Father*, Ten *Hail Marys*,
One *Glory Be*, etc.

Fruit of the Mystery: ***Trust in Mary's Intercession***

The Volumes

Direction for Our Times
as given to Anne, a lay apostle

Volume One: *Thoughts on Spirituality*

Volume Two: *Conversations with the*
                      Eucharistic Heart of Jesus

Volume Three: *God the Father Speaks to*
                      His Children
                      The Blessed Mother Speaks
                      to Her Bishops and Priests

Volume Four: *Jesus the King*
                      Heaven Speaks to Priests
                      Jesus Speaks to Sinners

Volume Five: *Jesus the Redeemer*

Volume Six: *Heaven Speaks to Families*

Volume Seven: *Greetings from Heaven*

Volume Eight: *Resting in the Heart of the Savior*

Volume Nine: *Angels*

Volume Ten: *Jesus Speaks to His Apostles*

Jesus Speaks to You - booklet containing the messages taken
from Volume Four- Part Three: Jesus Speaks to Sinners.

The Volumes are now available in PDF format
for free download and printing from our website:
www.directionforourtimes.org.
We encourage everyone to print and distribute them.

The Volumes are also available at your local bookstore.

The "Heaven Speaks" Booklets
Direction for Our Times
as given to Anne, a lay apostle

The following booklets are available individually from Direction for Our Times:

Heaven Speaks About Abortion
Heaven Speaks About Addictions
Heaven Speaks to Victims of Clerical Abuse
Heaven Speaks to Consecrated Souls
Heaven Speaks About Depression
Heaven Speaks About Divorce
Heaven Speaks to Prisoners
Heaven Speaks to Soldiers
Heaven Speaks About Stress
Heaven Speaks to Young Adults

Heaven Speaks to Those Away from the Church
Heaven Speaks to Those Considering Suicide
Heaven Speaks to Those Who Do Not Know Jesus
Heaven Speaks to Those Who Are Dying
Heaven Speaks to Those Who Experience Tragedy
Heaven Speaks to Those Who Fear Purgatory
Heaven Speaks to Those Who Have Rejected God
Heaven Speaks to Those Who Struggle to Forgive
Heaven Speaks to Those Who Suffer from Financial Need
Heaven Speaks to Parents Who Worry About
   Their Children's Salvation

All twenty of the "Heaven Speaks" booklets are now available for free download and printing from our website www.directionforourtimes.org. We encourage everyone to print and distribute these booklets.

Heaven Speaks Collection - Contains all 20 Heaven Speaks booklets.

Other Written Works by Anne, a lay apostle

Climbing the Mountain

This book contains the fascinating story of how the rescue mission began and how it has blossomed into a worldwide apostolate under the watchful eye and in complete obedience to the Church. It is the story of The Lay Apostolate of Jesus Christ the Returning King.

Also featured is a summary of Anne's mystical experiences of Heaven. She describes the heavenly home that has been created for God's children. Reading these accounts, you will learn that in Heaven we will experience constant unity with Jesus. Anne also confirms that souls in Heaven work together to assist in answering the prayers of God's earthly children. At one point in time Jesus tells Anne, ***"...you are a child of God and you have every right to be here."***

In the section entitled "Climbing the Mountain," Anne writes about her vision of the personal call to holiness that we all must hear.

It concludes with a reprint of the first ten "Heaven Speaks" booklets: Abortion, Addictions, Victims of Clerical Abuse, Consecrated Souls, Depression, Divorce, Prisoners, Soldiers, Stress, and Young Adults.

This is a book to be treasured as it reveals the intimate love of the Savior for each soul. Every reader will be called to great rejoicing, for truly, God's Kingdom comes.

The Mist of Mercy

Anne begins this book by telling us that the enemy of God is present on earth and a battle is being waged for souls. Satan is trying to destroy God's plan for us, which is unity with Him in Heaven for eternity. We must be alert to these efforts and be armed for the battle. This is the reality of spiritual warfare.

Following is a section entitled *Snapshots of Reality* which is a collection of short stories depicting realistic earthly struggles while including a glimpse of these same situations from the heavenly perspective and how our friends, the saints, act on our behalf more than we can imagine.

Also in this book is Anne's account of her mystical experiences of Purgatory. She tells us of the souls she saw there and describes the prayers they prayed and the remorse they felt for the choices they had made on earth which were against the will of God. You will be happy to learn that Purgatory is a great mercy of God and allows each soul there the perfect experience of preparation for eternity in Heaven.

The last section is a reprint of the Monthly Messages from Jesus Christ dated from December 1, 2004 through June 1, 2006.

Serving in Clarity

This book could be described as the guidebook for lay apostles who wish to serve Jesus Christ the Returning King. In essence, it is the walking guide, given to us by Heaven, describing how to obtain clarity so that our path up the Mountain of Holiness can be clearly identified.

The writing includes locutions from Jesus and Mary, encouraging us to trust that Heaven is sending extraordinary graces so that we will say "yes" to helping Jesus usher in the Age of Obedience.

Anne then shares her insight on how we should live our lives in love, holiness and obedience to the Church. Also included are vignettes of real life challenges that priests and people faced while serving in their vocations.

Especially compelling is the description of Anne's mystical experiences of the Mountain of Holiness, where Jesus showed her the current condition of the world so that lay apostles would be encouraged to participate in God's rescue mission for souls.

Reprinted in this book is *In Defense of Obedience and Reflections on the Priesthood,* as well as the Monthly Messages from Jesus dated July 26 through June 2008.

Serving in Clarity is a gift for all those who are serious about learning God's will for their life.

Lessons in Love

Lessons in Love highlights the importance of loving others with the unconditional love that Jesus has for each one of us. Anne illuminates a hopeful path of loving the people Jesus has placed in our lives. In particular, she shares her thoughts on the sacramental call to marriage and offers points for consideration when choosing a mate. She gives suggestions to navigate predictable marital difficulties and challenges. Also included is a series of thoughts for those living with homosexuality.

We learn about the place of the divine will. We read about the fruits of the renewal in which we are all asked to participate. Anne discuses some frequently asked questions regarding our Catholic faith, guiding us in our interactions with non-Christians. The book concludes with a reprint of five "Heaven Speaks" booklets.

Includes:
- The Place of the Divine Will
- Visions
- God is Love
- Marriage
- Questions and Answers
- Intimacy
- "Heaven Speaks" Booklets

In Defense of Obedience
and
Reflections on the Priesthood

This work by Anne consists of two essays on topics close to the heart of Jesus. The first is entitled *In Defense of Obedience* and the second is entitled *Reflections on the Priesthood.*

In Defense of Obedience is a serious call to return to a spirit of obedience to the Magisterium of the Church. Obedience to the Church is a must for every apostle, laity and clergy alike.

Anne's essay on the priesthood gives us the smallest glimpse of the love our Lord has for the men who hear and answer His call. We read the depth of the connection Jesus has with these men and how they are united in a most unique way to the Sacred Heart of Jesus and the Immaculate Heart of Mary. This is also a gentle reminder that we are called to love and support our priests who serve us in their humanity but with a heavenly dignity bestowed upon them from heaven by Jesus Christ, the First Priest.

Whispers from the Cross

In this book, Anne highlights the value of contemplating the Crucified Christ.

"Every lover of Jesus Christ will eventually find his way to the foot of the cross, where he will gaze at the Crucified One and engage in contemplation of those wounds which delivered salvation to humanity. Through contemplation of these wounds, we find our own place in the salvation story."

Anne identifies some of the temptations we experience during our service to Christ. She explores the importance of the vertical relationship with Christ that is central to the success of our service in our individual vocations and in the Church. Anne encourages us to accept the crosses we experience in our earthly journeys and also to accept the crosses God wills for those around us.

"Whispers from the Cross will direct us and correct us. These divine emanations from our Crucified King will console us and give us courage… In circumstances of suffering and pain we will feel strength because we arrive daily at the foot of the Cross to receive, and then offer, what is Jesus, instead of what is our feeble and changeable humanity."

Jesus Speaks to Children
and
Mary, Our Blessed Mother, Speaks to Children

These two books contain messages taken from Volume Six. They are beautiful messages to children from Jesus and Mary, Our Blessed Mother. Jesus and Mary teach and encourage children to grow closer to them. Concepts of growing in holiness are put into loving words that are easy for children to understand. The messages are accompanied by beautiful illustrations of Jesus, Mary and children together.

This book is part of a non-profit mission. Our Lord has requested that we spread these words internationally. Please help us.

In Ireland:
Direction For Our Times
The Hague Building
Cullies
Cavan
County Cavan

+353-(0)49-437-3040
contactus@dfot.ie

Registered Charity CHY17298

In the USA:
Direction For Our Times
9000 West 81st Street
Justice, Illinois 60458

708-496-9300
contactus@directionfor
ourtimes.org

A 501(c)(3) Organization

Adult Faith Formation

We are currently offering Adult Faith Formation programs. Please check our website for our most recent events including weekend retreats and our annual School of Holiness held each summer in Ireland. To learn more about these programs please contact one of our offices.